SHE STOOPS TO CONQUER

OR

THE MISTAKES OF A NIGHT

A Comedy

by

DR GOLDSMITH

D1494131

Samuel French — London
New York - Toronto - Hollywood

ISBN 0 573 01413 2

INTRODUCTION

GOLDSMITH doubtless wrote *She Stoops to Conquer* in 1771, for in a letter of his to Bennett Langton, dated September 7th of that year, he writes:

MY DEAR SIR

Since I had the pleasure of seeing you last, I have been almost wholly in the country, at a farmer's house quite alone, trying to write a comedy. It is now finished, but when or how it will be acted, or whether it will be acted at all, are questions I cannot resolve.

Every soul is a visiting about and merry but myself. And that is hard, too, as I have been trying these three months to do something to make people laugh. . . .

The farm-house stood on a gentle eminence in what is called Hyde Lane, near to the six-mile stone on the Edgware Road, and he occupied his apartment here till the period of his death, though still preserving his char bers in the Temple. The spot was well chosen, for few places near a great metropolis are prettier. From the commencement of the theatrical season 1772–3 he was anxiously endeavouring to procure a representation of his comedy, and in the first instance, it was placed in the hands of Colman, then manager of Covent Garden, but, after a considerable interval, returned by him. It was then submitted to Garrick, who displayed his usual aversion to give a plain answer, and neither a distinct yea or nay could be extracted from him. In this state of suspense Dr Johnson and other friends of the author again intervened with Colman, who, after urgent solicitations, yielded reluctant assent to its being brought forward at his theatre. It may be interesting here to insert two letters from Goldsmith to Garrick and Colman, without date, but no doubt written in January and February of 1773.

To DAVID GARRICK ESQ

DEAR SIR

I ask many pardons for the trouble I gave you yesterday. Upon more mature deliberation, and the advice of a sensible friend, I began to think it indelicate in me to throw upon you the odium of confirming Mr Colman's sentence. I therefore request you will send my play back by my servant, for having been assured of having it acted at the other house, though I confess yours in every respect more to my wish, yet it would be folly in me to forego an advantage which lies in my power of appealing from Mr Colman's opinion to the judgment of the town. I entreat, if not too late, you will keep this affair a secret for some time.

I am, dear Sir, your very humble Servant

OLIVER GOLDSMITH

To George Colman Esq

Dear Sir

I entreat you'll relieve me from that state of suspense in which I have been kept for a long time. Whatever objections you have made or shall make to my play I will endeavour to remove, and not argue about them. To bring in any new judges, either of its merits or faults, I can never submit to. Upon a former occasion, when my other play was before Mr Garrick, he offered to bring me before Mr Whitehead's tribunal, but I refused the proposal with indignation. I hope I shall not experience as hard treatment from you as from him. I have, as you know, a large sum of money to make up shortly; by accepting my play I can readily satisfy my creditor that way; at any rate, I must look about to some certainty to be prepared. For God's sake take the play, and let us make the best of it, and let me have the same measure at least which you have given as bad plays as mine.

> I am, your friend and Servant
> OLIVER GOLDSMITH

Dr Johnson, writing to Boswell in February, 1773, says: "Dr Goldsmith has a new comedy, which is expected in the spring. No name is yet given it. The chief diversion arises from a stratagem by which a lover is made to mistake his future father-in-law's house for an inn. This, you see, borders upon farce. The dialogue is quick and gay, and the incidents are so prepared as not to seem improbable." Again, on March 4th, he writes: "Dr Goldsmith has a new comedy in rehearsal at Covent Garden, to which the manager predicts ill success. I hope he will be mistaken. I think it deserves a very kind reception."

At first there was a difficulty in giving a name to the comedy. Dr Johnson remarks, "We are all in labour for a name to Goldy's play." The first adopted, but soon dismissed, was "The Old House a New Inn". Sir Joshua Reynolds proposed the "Belle's Stratagem", afterwards chosen by Mrs Cowley for one of her comedies. The present name, a suggestion of the author, was fixed on only three days before the representation, and in some of the newspapers it was announced simply as *The Mistakes of a Night*.

It was on March 15th, 1773, that Oliver Goldsmith's comedy, *She Stoops to Conquer* was produced at Covent Garden, and the original cast was as follows:

MR HARDCASTLE	.	.	. *Shuter*
YOUNG MARLOW	.	.	. *Lewes*
HASTINGS .	.	.	. *Du Bellamy*
TONY LUMPKIN .	.	.	. *Quick*
MRS HARDCASTLE	.	.	. *Mrs Green*
MISS HARDCASTLE	.	.	. *Mrs Bulkley*
MISS NEVILLE .	.	.	. *Mrs Kniveton*

It is the comedy of this period which of all others has survived to the present time, and remains one of the stock pieces of the English stage. It has been well said that there is nothing in it of the mawkishness of Kelly nor of the pompous affectation of Cumberland. Sentimental comedy had been the fashion, and though severely ridiculed by Foote at the Haymarket, in his *Handsome Housemaid; or, Piety in Patterns*, it was *She Stoops to Conquer* that really dealt the death blow, and restored to the town a hearty relish for a laugh. With all its faults and improbabilities, it is universally admitted this comedy is worth fifty cold, correct, still-life pieces. Colman was then manager; at first he refused the piece, but Dr Johnson stood manfully by Goldsmith, and owing to his influence the piece was put into rehearsal.

Cumberland relates of the first performance: "On the day of performance, Goldsmith's friends assembled in a considerable body at the Shakespeare Tavern for an early dinner. Dr Johnson took the chair at the head of a long table, and was in inimitable glee; they did not, however, forget their duty, and though they had better comedy going, in which Johnson was chief actor, they betook themselves in good time to their separate and allotted posts, having preconcerted signals for plaudits in a manner that gave every one his cue, where to look for them, and how to follow them up. One of the company was Adam Drummond, who was gifted by nature with the most sonorous and at the same time most contagious laugh that ever echoed from the human lungs; he ingenuously, however, confessed that he knew no more when to give his fire than the cannon did that was placed on a battery; he desired, therefore, to have a flapper at his elbow, and I was deputed to that office. All eyes were upon Dr Johnson, who sat in the front row of a side box, and when he laughed everybody thought himself warranted to roar; in the meantime, Drummond followed signals with a rattle so irresistibly comic that, when he had repeated it several times, the attention of the spectators was so engrossed by his person and performances, that the progress of the play seemed likely to become a secondary object, and I found it prudent to insinuate to him that he might halt his music without any prejudice to the author; but, alas, it was now too late to rein him in. He had laughed upon my signal where he found no joke, and now he unluckily fancied he found a joke in almost everything that was said, so that nothing in nature could be more malapropos than some of his bursts every now and then were. These were dangerous moments, for the pit began to take umbrage; however, the author's friends carried his play through triumphantly, and their manœuvres were attended with complete success."

Cumberland's story is, however, doubtful. It was written from memory at the distance of thirty years after the transaction. Northcote says the dinner took place at Sir Joshua Reynolds's, and Mr Fitzherbert, who was represented to be one of the party, had died the preceding year. Goldsmith's friends, Johnson, Burke, Reynolds, Dr Franklin, Kelly, Macpherson, and others, were no doubt present, willing to promote his success; but such advocates can never overpower the popular voice. Should ever a first night succeed by such means, the second or third will show the failure; whereas, every succeeding representation of *She Stoops to Conquer* only served to raise its popularity.

Immediately after the production Goldsmith writes to his friend, Mr Craddock:—

To Mr Craddock

My dear Sir

The play has met with a success much beyond your expectations or mine. I thank you sincerely for your epilogue, which, however, could not be used, but, with your permission, shall be printed. The story, in short, is this—Murphy sent me rather the outline of an epilogue than an epilogue, which was to be sung by Mrs Catley, and which she approved. Mrs Bulkley, hearing this, insisted on throwing up her part, unless, according to the custom of the theatre, she were permitted to speak the epilogue. In this embarrassment I thought of making a quarrelling epilogue between Catley and her, debating who should speak the epilogue, but then Mrs Catley refused after I had taken the trouble of drawing it out. I was then at a loss indeed. An epilogue was to be made, and for none but Mrs Bulkley. I made one, and Colman thought it too bad to be spoken; I was obliged therefore to try a fourth time, and I made a very mawkish thing, as you'll shortly see. Such is the history of my stage adventures, and which I have at last done with. I cannot help saying that I am very sick of the stage, and though I believe I shall get three tolerable benefits, yet I shall, on the whole, be a loser, even in a pecuniary light; my ease and comfort I certainly lost while it was in agitation.

I am, my dear Craddock
Your obliged and obedient Servant,
Oliver Goldsmith

P.S.—Present my most humble respects to Mrs Craddock.

Johnson also, when Boswell was present, on *She Stoops to Conquer* being mentioned, said: "I know of no comedy for many years that has so much exhilarated an audience, that has answered so much the great end of comedy—making an audience merry." On the 13th April, Boswell writes: "We drank tea with the ladies at General Oglethorp's, and Goldsmith sang Tony Lumpkin's song in his comedy *She Stoops to Conquer*—and a very pretty one—to an Irish tune, *The Humours of Ballamagairy*, which he had designed for Miss Hardcastle, but as Mrs Bulkley, who played the part, could not sing, it was left out."

Northcote, the famous painter, then a young man and residing with Sir Joshua Reynolds, wrote to his brother, March 24th, 1773: "Last Monday I went to see Goldsmith's new play, and, quite the reverse to everybody's expectation, it was received with the utmost applause, and Garrick has writ a very excellent prologue to it in ridicule of the late sentimental comedies. Goldsmith was so kind as to offer me half-a-dozen tickets for the play on his night, and I intend to accept two or three. He is going to dedicate his play to old Johnson."

When *She Stoops to Conquer* was first put in rehearsal, Gentleman Smith threw up young Marlow, Woodward refused Tony Lumpkin, and Mrs Abingdon—greatest mortification of all—declined Miss Hardcastle. Great was the alarm amongst Goldsmith's friends, to whom, however, he replied, "No! I'd rather my play were damned by bad players than merely saved by good acting"; and so Tony was cast to Quick, who had played the small part of the Postboy in *The Good-Natured Man*, to Shuter was given Mr Hardcastle, and on his protesting in his vehement odd way hat Lewes, who was harlequin in the theatre, "could patter and use the gob-box as quick and smart as any of them", Goldsmith consented he should appear as Young Marlow. Du Bellamy, Green, and Mrs Bulkley completed the cast.

Of the first cast, Shuter, the Mr Hardcastle, was on the stage from 1744 to 1776, and played throughout the entire range of a wide comic repertory. Off as on the stage, it was Shuter's characteristic that he pleased everybody and ruined himself. Fitzgerald says of him: "There was Shuter, who it was said Mr Garrick pronounced the greatest comic genius he had ever seen." He commenced his vocation as Catesby, at Richmond, concluding as Falstaff (played for his own benefit) at Covent Garden, in May, 1776.

Lewes, who had played with success in Dublin and Edinburgh, came to London and Covent Garden in 1773. Here, when ill, many of Barry's chief characters were entrusted to him. He remained at Covent Garden till 1809, when he took farewell of the stage in the *Copper Captain*, the best of all his parts. He was famed as one of the most delightful performers of his class, and retained to the last his invincible airiness and juvenility. Leigh Hunt saw him take leave of the public a man of sixty-five looking not more than half the age, and heard him say, in a voice broken by emotion, that "for the space of thirty years he had not once incurred their displeasure". He died in 1813, and out of part of his fortune bequeathed to his sister the beautiful new church at Ealing was chiefly erected.

Quick, who played Mr Hardcastle's stepson, loved to sit and talk of Garrick and Goldsmith, and what the dramatist said to him when he enacted Tony Lumpkin on the first night of the production of *She Stoops to Conquer*. He was born in 1748, and left his father, a brewer, when only fourteen years of age to become an actor, and after a varied experience in Surrey and Kent, we find him at the Haymarket, in 1769, a great favourite of King George III who, when visiting the theatre, always expected Quick to appear in a prominent character. He was the original Acres, as well as Tony Lumpkin. In 1798, he quitted the stage with over £10,000 of savings.

Mrs Green, Hippisley's daughter and Governor Hippisley's sister, not only was the original Mrs Hardcastle, but also the original Mrs Malaprop. Her public career began in 1730 and closed in 1779. It is said of her that she possessed humour even to drollery, combining the unctuousness of Shuter with the quaintness of her father.

The Miss Hardcastle was Mrs Bulkley, the Miss Wilford of earlier days. She played at Edinburgh for a season, and her Lady Racket was talked over by the Scotch beaux at the beginning of this century with their hands on their hearts and over their waistcoat pockets. She also played in *The Rivals* on its production, and was the original Julia. She remained on the London stage from 1764 to 1789, and at the time of her death had become Mrs Baresford.

On its first appearance, the comedy was enacted twelve times, the tenth night was by royal command; and the author's nights were supposed to have realized between four and five hundred pounds. Foote acted it in the summer at the Haymarket, and it was resumed with the re-opening of Covent Garden in the winter, and again had the compliment of a royal command.

She Stoops to Conquer was played subsequently at the Haymarket in 1777, and the occasion is chiefly memorable from the circumstance that Miss Farren, afterwards Countess of Derby, made her first appearance in London as Miss Hardcastle. She soon became a great favourite with the public. In 1774 she had acted Columbine at Wakefield and sung between the acts. She was still so young, in the season when she came to Drury Lane, Mrs Robinson says, that most of the principal parts were performed by four actresses under twenty, viz, herself, Miss Farren, Miss Walpole, and Miss P. Hopkins.

In 1825 we find the comedy was revived at Covent Garden, and Robert Keeley was the Tony Lumpkin; whilst Miss Maria Foote, afterwards Countess of Harrington, appeared as Miss Hardcastle. John Fawcett, whom Boaden described as "a great original masterly comedian, always natural and extremely powerful", was Mr Hardcastle; Richard Jones, the successor and protégé of Lewes, Young Marlow; and the respected and cheerful Mrs Davenport played again the part in which she had made her London début of Mrs Hardcastle.

Since this period it has been very often played, and remains, as it will always remain throughout the country, a stock piece of the English stage.

To

SAMUEL JOHNSON, LL.D.

BY inscribing this slight performance to you, I do not mean so much to compliment you as myself. It may do me some honour to inform the public that I have lived many years in intimacy with you. It may serve the interests of mankind also to inform them that the greatest wit may be found in a character without impairing the most unaffected piety.

I have, particularly, reason to thank you for your partiality to this performance. The undertaking a comedy not merely sentimental was very dangerous; and Mr Colman, who saw this piece in its various stages, always thought it so. However, I ventured to trust it to the public; and, though it was necessarily delayed till late in the season, I have every reason to be grateful.

I am, Dear Sir,
Your most sincere friend
and admirer,
OLIVER GOLDSMITH.

PROLOGUE

By David Garrick Esq.

(Enter Mr Woodward, *dressed in black, and holding a handkerchief to his eyes)*

Excuse me, sirs, I pray—I can't yet speak—
I'm crying now—and have been all the week!
'Tis not alone this mourning suit, good masters;
I've that within—for which there are no plasters!
Pray would you know the reason why I'm crying?
The Comic Muse, long sick, is now a dying!
And if she goes, my tears will never stop;
For as a player, I can't squeeze out one drop:
I am undone, that's all—shall lose my bread—
I'd rather, but that's nothing—lose my head.
When the sweet maid is laid upon the bier,
Shuter and *I* shall be chief mourners here.
To *her* a mawkish drab of spurious breed,
Who deals in *sentimentals,* will succeed!
Poor *Ned* and *I* are dead to all intents,
We can as soon speak *Greek* as *sentiments!*
Both nervous grown, to keep our spirits up,
We now and then take down a hearty cup.
What shall we do?—If Comedy forsake us!
They'll turn us out, and no-one else will take us:
But why can't I be moral?—Let me try—
My heart thus pressing—fixed my face and eye—
With a sententious look, that nothing means
(Faces are blocks in sentimental scenes)
Thus I begin—*All is not gold that glitters,*
Pleasure seems sweet, but proves a glass of bitters.
When ign'rance enters, folly is at hand;
Learning is better far than house and land.
Let not your virtue trip, who trips may stumble,
And virtue is not virtue, if she tumble.
  I give it up—morals won't do for me;
To make you laugh I must play tragedy.
One hope remains—hearing the maid was ill,
A *doctor* comes this night to show his skill.
To cheer her heart, and give your muscles motion,
He in *five draughts* prepared, presents a potion:
A kind of magic charm—for be assured,
If you will *swallow* it, the maid is cured.

x

But desp'rate the doctor, and her case is,
If you reject the dose, and make wry faces!
This truth he boasts, will boast it while he lives,
No *pois'nous drugs* are mixed in what he gives;
Should he succeed, you'll give him his degree;
If not, within he will receive no fee!
The college, *you*, must his pretensions back,
Pronounce him *regular*, or dub him quack.

CHARACTERS

(in order of appearance)

MRS HARDCASTLE
MR HARDCASTLE
TONY LUMPKIN, his stepson
KATE HARDCASTLE
CONSTANCE NEVILLE, Kate's cousin
LANDLORD
MARLOW
HASTINGS
DIGGORY⎫
ROGER ⎭servants to Mr Hardcastle
SIR CHARLES MARLOW, Marlow's father
SERVANTS, FELLOWS, MAID, etc.

SCENES

ACT I—SCENE 1		Hardcastle's house
	SCENE 2	*The Three Pigeons*
ACT II		Hardcastle's house
ACT III		The same
ACT IV		The same
ACT V—SCENE 1		The same
	SCENE 2	The garden of the house
	SCENE 3	Hardcastle's house

The music for the song *The Three Pigeons* on page 6 may be obtained from Samuel French Ltd.

SHE STOOPS TO CONQUER

ACT I

Scene 1

Scene—*A chamber in Mr Hardcastle's house.*

As the Curtain *rises,* Mr *and* Mrs Hardcastle *enter* R.

Mrs Hardcastle. I vow, Mr Hardcastle, you're very particular. Is there a creature in the whole country, but ourselves, that does not take a trip to town now and then, to rub off the rust a little? There's the two Miss Hoggs, and our neighbour, Mrs Grigsby, go to take a month's polishing every winter.

Hardcastle. Ay, and bring back vanity and affectation to last them the whole year. I wonder why London cannot keep its own fools at home. In my time, the follies of the town crept slowly among us, but now they travel faster than a stage-coach. Its fopperies come down, not only as inside passengers, but in the very basket.

Mrs Hardcastle. Ay, your times were fine times indeed; you have been telling us of them for many a long year. Here we live in an old rumbling mansion, that looks for all the world like an inn, but that we never see company. Our best visitors are old Mrs Oddfish, the curate's wife, and little Cripplegate, the lame dancing-master; and all our entertainment, your old stories of Prince Eugene and the Duke of Marlborough. I hate such old-fashioned trumpery.

Hardcastle. And I love it. I love everything that's old: old friends, old times, old manners, old books, old wine; and I believe, Dorothy (*taking her hand*), you'll own I have been pretty fond of an old wife.

Mrs Hardcastle. Lord, Mr Hardcastle, you're for ever at your Dorothy's, and your old wife's! You may be a Darby, but I'll be no Joan, I promise you. I'm not so old as you would make me by more than one good year. Add twenty to twenty, and make money of that.

Hardcastle. Let me see; twenty added to twenty makes just fifty and seven.

Mrs Hardcastle. It's false, Mr Hardcastle: I was but twenty when I was brought to bed of Tony, that I had by Mr Lumpkin, my first husband; and he's not come to years of discretion yet.

Hardcastle. Nor ever will, I dare answer for him. Ay, you have taught *him* finely.

I

MRS HARDCASTLE. No matter; Tony Lumpkin has a good fortune. My son is not to live by his learning. I don't think a boy wants much learning to spend fifteen hundred a year.

HARDCASTLE. Learning, quotha! A mere composition of tricks and mischief.

MRS HARDCASTLE. Humour, my dear: nothing but humour. Come, Mr Hardcastle, you must allow the boy a little humour.

HARDCASTLE. I'd sooner allow him a horse-pond. If burning the footmen's shoes, frighting the maids, and worrying the kittens, be humour, he has it. It was but yesterday he fastened my wig to the back of my chair, and when I went to make a bow, I popped my bald head in Mrs Frizzle's face.

MRS HARDCASTLE. And am I to blame? The poor boy was always too sickly to do any good. A school would be his death. When he comes to be a little stronger, who knows what a year or two's Latin may do for him?

HARDCASTLE. Latin for him! A cat and fiddle! No, no, the alehouse and the stable are the only schools he'll ever go to.

MRS HARDCASTLE. Well, we must not snub the poor boy now, for I believe we shan't have him long among us. Anybody that looks in his face may see he's consumptive.

HARDCASTLE. Ay, if growing too fat be one of the symptoms.

MRS HARDCASTLE. He coughs sometimes.

HARDCASTLE. Yes, when his liquor goes the wrong way.

MRS HARDCASTLE. I'm actually afraid of his lungs.

HARDCASTLE. And truly so am I; for he sometimes whoops like a speaking-trumpet.

(TONY *halloos off stage* R)

O there he goes—a very consumptive figure truly.

(TONY LUMPKIN *enters* R, *crossing the stage*)

MRS HARDCASTLE. Tony, where are you going, my charmer? Won't you give papa and I a little of your company, lovee?

TONY. I'm in haste, mother, I can't stay.

MRS HARDCASTLE. You shan't venture out this raw evening, my dear; you look most shockingly.

TONY. I can't stay, I tell you. *The Three Pigeons* expects me down every moment. There's some fun going forward.

HARDCASTLE. Ay; the alehouse, the old place: I thought so.

MRS HARDCASTLE. A low, paltry set of fellows.

TONY. Not so low, neither. There's Dick Muggins the Exciseman, Jack Slang the horse doctor, little Aminadab that grinds the music box, and Tom Twist that spins the pewter platter.

MRS HARDCASTLE. Pray, my dear, disappoint them for one night at least.

TONY. As for disappointing *them*, I should not so much mind; but I can't abide to disappoint *myself*.

Mrs Hardcastle (*detaining him*) You shan't go.
Tony. I will, I tell you.
Mrs Hardcastle. I say you shan't.
Tony. We'll see which is strongest, you or I.

(Tony *exits* l, *hauling* Mrs Hardcastle *out*)

Hardcastle. Ay, there goes a pair that only spoil each other. But is not the whole age in a combination to drive sense and discretion out of doors? There's my pretty darling Kate; the fashions of the times have almost infected her too. By living a year or two in town, she is as fond of gauze, and French frippery, as the best of them.

(Miss Hardcastle *enters* r)

Blessings on my pretty innocence! Dressed out as usual, my Kate. Goodness! What a quantity of superfluous silk hast thou got about thee, girl! I could never teach the fools of this age that the indigent world could be clothed out of the trimmings of the vain.

Miss Hardcastle. You know our agreement, sir. You allow me the morning to receive and pay visits, and to dress in my own manner; and in the evening, I put on my housewife's dress to please you.

Hardcastle. Well, remember I insist on the terms of our agreement; and, by the bye, I believe I shall have occasion to try your obedience this every evening.

Miss Hardcastle. I protest, sir, I don't comprehend your meaning.

Hardcastle. Then to be plain with you, Kate, I expect the young gentleman I have chosen to be your husband from town this very day. I have his father's letter, in which he informs me his son is set out, and that he intends to follow him shortly after.

Miss Hardcastle. Indeed! I wish I had known something of this before. Bless me, how shall I behave? It's a thousand to one I shan't like him; our meeting will be so formal, and so like a thing of business, that I shall find no room for friendship or esteem.

Hardcastle. Depend upon it, child, I'll never control your choice; but Mr Marlow, whom I have pitched upon, is the son of my old friend, Sir Charles Marlow, of whom you have heard me talk so often. The young gentleman has been bred a scholar, and is designed for an employment in the service of his country. I am told he's a man of an excellent understanding.

Miss Hardcastle. Is he?
Hardcastle. Very generous.
Miss Hardcastle. I believe I shall like him.
Hardcastle. Young and brave.
Miss Hardcastle. I'm sure I shall like him.
Hardcastle. And very handsome.

MISS HARDCASTLE. My dear papa, say no more (*she kisses his hand*); he's mine. I'll have him.

HARDCASTLE. And to crown all, Kate, he's one of the most bashful and reserved young fellows in all the world.

MISS HARDCASTLE. Eh! You have frozen me to death again. That word reserved has undone all the rest of his accomplishments. A reserved lover, it is said, always makes a suspicious husband.

HARDCASTLE. On the contrary, modesty seldom resides in a breast that is not enriched with nobler virtues. It was the very feature in his character that first struck me.

MISS HARDCASTLE. He must have more striking features to catch me, I promise you. However, if he be so young, so handsome, and so everything as you mention, I believe he'll do still. I think I'll have him.

HARDCASTLE. Ay, Kate, but there is still an obstacle. It's more than an even wager he may not have *you*.

MISS HARDCASTLE. My dear papa, why will you mortify one so? Well, if he refuses, instead of breaking my heart at his indifference, I'll only break my glass for its flattery, set my cap to some newer fashion, and look out for some less difficult admirer.

HARDCASTLE. Bravely resolved! In the meantime I'll go and prepare the servants for his reception; as we seldom see company, they want as much training as a company of recruits the first day's muster.

(HARDCASTLE *exits* L)

MISS HARDCASTLE. Lud, this news of papa's puts me all in a flutter! Young, handsome—these he puts last, but I put them foremost. Sensible, good-natured—I like all that. But then reserved, and sheepish; that's much against him. Yet can't he be cured of his timidity by being taught to be proud of his wife? Yes, and can't I—but I vow I'm disposing of the husband before I have secured the lover.

(MISS NEVILLE *enters* L)

I'm glad you're come, Neville, my dear. Tell me, Constance, how do I look this evening? Is there anything whimsical about me? Is it one of my well-looking days, child? Am I in face today?

MISS NEVILLE. Perfectly, my dear. Yet now I look again— bless me!—sure no accident has happened among the canary birds or the gold-fishes? Has your brother or the cat been meddling? Or has the last novel been too moving?

MISS HARDCASTLE. No; nothing of all this. I have been threatened—I can scarce get it out—I have been threatened with a lover.

MISS NEVILLE. And his name .

MISS HARDCASTLE. Is Marlow.

MISS NEVILLE. Indeed!

MISS HARDCASTLE. The son of Sir Charles Marlow.

MISS NEVILLE. As I live, the most intimate friend of Mr Hastings, *my* admirer. They are never asunder. I believe you must have seen him when we lived in town.

MISS HARDCASTLE. Never.

MISS NEVILLE. He's a very singular character, I assure you. Among women of reputation and virtue, he is the modestest man alive; but his acquaintance give him a very different character among creatures of another stamp: you understand me.

MISS HARDCASTLE. An odd character, indeed! I shall never be able to manage him. What shall I do? Pshaw, think no more of him, but trust to occurrences for success. But how goes on your own affair, my dear, has my mother been courting you for my brother Tony, as usual?

MISS NEVILLE. I have just come from one of our agreeable *tête-à-têtes*. She has been saying a hundred tender things, and setting off her pretty monster as the very pink of perfection.

MISS HARDCASTLE. And her partiality is such, that she actually thinks him so. A fortune like yours is no small temptation; besides, as she has the sole management of it, I'm not surprised to see her unwilling to let it go out of the family.

MISS NEVILLE. A fortune like mine, which chiefly consists in jewels, is no such mighty temptation. But at any rate, if my dear Hastings be but constant, I make no doubt to be too hard for her at last. However, I let her suppose that I am in love with her son, and she never once dreams that my affections are fixed upon another.

MISS HARDCASTLE. My good brother holds out stoutly. I could almost love him for hating you so.

MISS NEVILLE. It is a good-natured creature at bottom, and I'm sure would wish to see me married to anybody but himself. But my aunt's bell rings for our afternoon's walk round the improvements. *Allons.* Courage is necessary, as our affairs are critical.

MISS HARDCASTLE. Would it were bedtime, and all were well.

(MISS HARDCASTLE *and* MISS NEVILLE *exit* L)

CURTAIN

SCENE 2

SCENE—*A room at "The Three Pigeons".*

When the CURTAIN *rises, several shabby* FELLOWS *are seated at a table, with punch and tobacco.* TONY *is at their head, a little higher than the rest: a mallet in his hand.*

OMNES. Hurrah, hurrah, hurrah, bravo!

1ST FELLOW. Now, gentlemen, silence for a song. The 'squire is going to knock himself down for a song!

OMNES. Ay, a song, a song!

TONY. Then I'll sing you, gentlemen, a song I made upon this alehouse, *The Three Pigeons.*

Song

Let schoolmasters puzzle their brain
    With grammar, and nonsense, and learning:
Good liquor, I stoutly maintain,
    Gives *genus* a better discerning.
Let them brag of their heathenish gods,
    Their Lethes, their Styxes, and Stygians;
Their *quis,* and their *quæs,* and their *quods,*
    They're all but a parcel of pigeons.
               Toroddle, toroddle, toroll.

When Methodist preachers come down,
    A-preaching that drinking is sinful,
I'll wager the rascals a crown,
    They always preach best with a skinful.
But when you come down with your pence,
    For a slice of their scurvy religion,
I'll leave it to all men of sense,
    But you, my good friend, are the pigeon.
               Toroddle, toroddle, toroll.

Then come, put the jorum about,
    And let us be merry and clever;
Our hearts and our liquors are stout;
    Here's *The Three Jolly Pigeons* for ever.
Let some cry up woodcock or hare,
    Your bustards, your ducks, and your widgeons;
But of all the birds in the air,
    Here's a health to *The Three Jolly Pigeons.*
               Toroddle, toroddle, toroll.

OMNES. Bravo, bravo!

1ST FELLOW. The 'squire has got spunk in him.

2ND FELLOW. I loves to hear him sing, bekeays he never gives us nothing that's low.

3RD FELLOW. Damn anything that's low; I cannot bear it.

4TH FELLOW. The genteel thing is the genteel thing at any time, if so be that a gentleman bees in a concatenation accordingly.

3RD FELLOW. I like the maxum of it, Master Muggins. What, though I am obligated to dance a bear, a man may be a gentleman for all that. May this be my poison if my bear ever dances but to the very genteelest of tunes—*Water parted*, or the minuet in *Ariadne*.

2ND FELLOW. What a pity it is the 'squire is not come to his own. It would be well for all the publicans within ten miles round of him.

TONY. Ecod, and so it would, Master Slang. I'd then show what it was to keep choice of company.

2ND FELLOW. Oh, he takes after his own father for that. To be sure, old 'Squire Lumpkin was the finest gentleman I ever set my eyes on. For winding the straight horn, or beating a thicket for a hare, or a wench, he never had his fellow. It was a saying in the place, that he kept the best horses, dogs, and girls in the whole country.

TONY. Ecod, and when I'm of age I'll be no bastard I promise you. I have been thinking of Bett Bouncer and the miller's grey mare to begin with. But come, my boys, drink about and be merry, for you pay no reckoning.

(*The* LANDLORD *enters* L)

Well, Stingo, what's the matter?

LANDLORD. There be two gentlemen, in a post chaise, at the door—they have lost their way upo' the forest, and they are talking something about Mr Hardcastle.

TONY. As sure as can be, one of them must be the gentleman that's coming down to court my sister. Do they seem to be Londoners?

LANDLORD. I believe they may. They look *woundily like Frenchmen.

TONY. Then desire them to step this way, and I'll set them right in a twinkling.

(*The* LANDLORD *exits* L)

Gentlemen, as they mayn't be good enough company for you, step down for a moment, and I'll be with you in the squeezing of a lemon.

(*The* FELLOWS *exit* L)

Father-in-law has been calling me a whelp, and hound, this half-year. Now if I pleased, I could be so revenged upon the old grumbletonian. But then I'm afraid—afraid of what? I shall soon be worth fifteen hundred a year, and let him frighten me out of *that* if he can.

(*The* LANDLORD *enters* L, *conducting* MARLOW *and* HASTINGS)

MARLOW. What a tedious uncomfortable day have we had of it! We were told it was but forty miles across the country, and we have come above threescore.

* Woundily, *i.e. very.*

HASTINGS. And all, Marlow, from that unaccountable reserve of yours, that would not let us inquire more frequently on the way.

MARLOW (LC) I own, Hastings, I am unwilling to lay myself under an obligation to every one I meet, and often stand the chance of an unmannerly answer.

HASTINGS (L) At present, however, we are not likely to receive any answer.

TONY (RC) No offence, gentlemen; but I'm told you have been inquiring for one Mr Hardcastle, in these parts. Do you know what part of the country you are in?

HASTINGS. Not in the least, sir, but should thank you for information.

TONY. Nor the way you came?

HASTINGS. No, sir; but if you can inform us . . .

TONY. Why, gentlemen, if you know neither the road you are going, nor where you are, nor the road you came, the first thing I have to inform you is that—you have lost your way.

MARLOW. We wanted no ghost to tell us that.

TONY. Pray, gentlemen, may I be so bold as to ask the place from whence you came?

MARLOW. That's not necessary towards directing us where we are to go.

TONY. No offence; but question for question is all fair, you know. Pray, gentleman, is not this same Hardcastle a cross-grain'd, old-fashion'd, whimsical fellow, with an ugly face, a daughter, and a pretty son?

HASTINGS. We have not seen the gentleman, but he has the family you mention.

TONY. The daughter a tall, trapesing, trolloping, talkative, maypole—the son a pretty, well-bred, agreeable youth, that everybody is fond of.

MARLOW. Our information differs in this; the daughter is said to be well-bred and beautiful; the son, an awkward booby, reared up and spoiled at his mother's apron-string.

TONY. He-he-hem—then, gentlemen, all I have to tell you is, that you won't reach Mr Hardcastle's house this night, I believe.

HASTINGS. Unfortunate!

TONY. It's a damn'd long, dark, boggy, dirty, dangerous way. Stingo, tell the gentlemen the way to Mr Hardcastle's. (*He winks to the Landlord, and moves* R) Mr Hardcastle's, of Quagmire Marsh; you understand me.

LANDLORD (C) Master Hardcastle's! Lack-a-daisy, my masters, you're come a deadly deal wrong! When you came to the bottom of the hill, you should have crossed down Squash Lane.

MARLOW. Cross down Squash Lane?

LANDLORD. Then you were to keep straightforward till you came to four roads.

Marlow. Come to where four roads meet?

Tony. Ay; but you must be sure to take only one of them.

Marlow. O, sir, you're facetious.

Tony. Then keeping to the right, you are to go sideways till you come upon Crackskull Common; there you must look sharp for the track of the wheel, and go forward till you come to farmer Murrain's barn. Coming to the farmer's barn you are to turn to the right, and then to the left, and then to the right-about again, till you find out the old mill . . .

Marlow. Zounds, man! we could as soon find out the longitude.

Hastings. What's to be done, Marlow?

Marlow. This house promises but a poor reception; though perhaps the landlord can accommodate us.

Landlord. Alack, master, we have but one spare bed in the whole house.

Tony. And, to my knowledge, that's taken up by three lodgers already. (*After a pause, in which the rest seem disconcerted*) I have hit it; don't you think, Stingo, our landlady could accommodate the gentlemen by the fireside with three chairs and a bolster?

Hastings. I hate sleeping by the fireside.

Marlow. And I detest your three chairs and a bolster.

Tony. You do, do you? Then let me see—what if you go on a mile further, to the *Buck's Head*, the old *Buck's Head*, on the hill, one of the best inns in the whole county.

Hastings. O, ho! So we have escaped an adventure for this night, however.

Landlord (*aside to Tony*) Sure you ben't sending them to your father's as an inn, be you?

Tony (*aside to the Landlord*) Mum, you fool you; let *them* find that out. (*To the others*) You have only to keep on straightforward till you come to a large old house by the road-side: you'll see a pair of large horns over the door, that's the sign: drive up the yard, and call stoutly about you.

Hastings. Sir, we are obliged to you. The servants can't miss the way?

Tony. No, no; but I tell you, though, the landlord is rich, and going to leave off business; so he wants to be thought a gentleman, saving your presence—he, he, he! He'll be for giving you his company, and, ecod, if you mind him, he'll persuade you that his mother was an alderman, and his aunt a justice of peace.

Landlord. A troublesome old blade, to be sure; but a keeps as good wines and beds as any in the whole country.

Marlow. Well, if he supplies us with these, we shall want no further connexion. We are to turn to the right, did you say?

Tony. No, no, straightforward. I'll just step myself, and show you a piece of the way. (*To the Landlord*) Mum.

(Tony, Marlow *and* Hastings *exit* l)

Landlord. Ah, bless your heart, for a sweet, pleasant—damn'd mischievous son of a whore.

The Landlord *exits* l *as—*

the Curtain *falls*

ACT II

SCENE—*Hardcastle's house.*

When the CURTAIN *rises,* HARDCASTLE *enters* R, *followed by* DIGGORY *and three or four awkward* SERVANTS. HARDCASTLE *stands* C, *the others move* R *and* L.

HARDCASTLE. Well, I hope you are perfect in the table exercise I have been teaching you these three days. You all know your posts and your places, and can show that you have been used to good company without ever stirring from home.

OMNES. Ay, ay!

HARDCASTLE. When company comes, you are not to pop out and stare, and then run in again, like frighted rabbits in a warren.

OMNES. No, no!

HARDCASTLE. You, Diggory, whom I have taken from the barn, are to make a show at the side table; and you, Roger, whom I have advanced from the plough, are to place yourself behind *my* chair. But you're not to stand so, with your hands in your pockets. Take your hands from your pockets, Roger, and from your head, you blockhead you. See how Diggory carries his hands. They're a little too stiff, indeed, but that's no great matter.

DIGGORY. Ay, mind how I hold them. I learned to hold my hands this way when I was upon drill for the militia; and so being upon drill . . .

HARDCASTLE. You must not be so talkative, Diggory; you must be all attention to the guests. You must hear us talk, and not think of talking; you must see us drink, and not think of drinking; you must see us eat, and not think of eating.

DIGGORY. By the laws, your worship, that's perfectly unpossible. Whenever Diggory sees yeating going forward, ecod, he's always wishing for a mouthful himself.

HARDCASTLE. Blockhead! Is not a bellyful in the kitchen as good as a bellyful in the parlour? Stay your stomach with that reflection.

DIGGORY. Ecod, I thank your worship. I'll make a shift to stay my stomach with a slice of cold beef in the pantry.

HARDCASTLE. Diggory, you are too talkative. Then, if I happen to say a good thing, or tell a good story at table, you must not all burst out a-laughing, as if you made part of the company.

DIGGORY. Then, ecod, your worship must not tell the story of Ould Grouse in the gun-room: I can't help laughing at that—he! he! he!—for the soul of me. We have laughed at that these twenty years—ha! ha! ha!

(*They all laugh*)

Hardcastle. Ha, ha, ha! The story is a good one. Well, honest Diggory, you may laugh at that; but still remember to be attentive. Suppose one of the company should call for a glass of wine—how will you behave? (*To Diggory*) A glass of wine, sir, if you please. Eh! Why don't you move?

Diggory. Ecod, your worship, I never have courage till I see the eatables and drinkables brought upo' the table, and then I'm as bauld as a lion.

Hardcastle. What, will nobody move?

1st Servant. I'm not to leave this pleace.

2nd Servant. I'm sure it's no pleace of mine.

3rd Servant. Nor mine, for sartain.

Diggory. *Wauns! and I'm sure it canna be mine.

Hardcastle. You numskulls! And so while, like your betters, you are quarrelling for places, the guests must be starved. O, you dunces! I find I must begin all over again. But don't I hear a coach drive into the yard? To your posts, you blockheads. I'll go in the meantime and give my old friend's son a hearty welcome at the gate.

(Hardcastle *exits* L)

Diggory. By the elevens, my place is gone quite out of my head.

(Diggory *exits* L)

Roger. I know that my place is to be everywhere.

1st Servant. Where the devil is mine?

2nd Servant. My place is to be nowhere at all; and so I'ze go about my business.

(*The* Servants *exit* R *and* L, *running about as if frightened.*
  A Servant *enters with candles, showing in* Marlow *and* Hastings)

Servant. Welcome, gentlemen, very welcome. This way.

Hastings. After the disappointments of the day, welcome once more, Charles, to the comforts of a clean room and a good fire. Upon my word, a very well-looking house—antique, but creditable.

Marlow. The usual fate of a large mansion. Having first ruined the master by good housekeeping, it at last comes to levy contributions as an inn.

Hastings. As you say, we passengers are to be taxed to pay all these fineries. I have often seen a good sideboard, or a marble chimney-piece, though not actually put in the bill, inflame a reckoning confoundedly.

* Wauns, *swounds, i.e. by God's wounds.*

MARLOW. Travellers, George, must pay in all places; the only difference is, that in good inns you pay dearly for luxuries—in bad inns you are fleeced and starved.

HASTINGS. You have lived pretty much among them. In truth, I have been often surprised that you who have seen so much of the world, with your natural good sense and your many opportunities, could never yet acquire a requisite share of assurance.

MARLOW. The Englishman's malady; but tell me, George, where could I have learned that assurance you talk of? My life has been chiefly spent in a college or an inn, in seclusion from that lovely part of the creation that chiefly teach men confidence. I don't know that I was ever familiarly acquainted with a single modest woman—except my mother. But among females of another class you know . . .

HASTINGS. Ay, among them you are impudent enough of all conscience.

MARLOW. They are of *us*, you know.

HASTINGS. But in the company of women of reputation I never saw such an idiot, such a trembler; you look for all the world as if you wanted an opportunity of stealing out of the room.

MARLOW. Why, man, that's because I *do* want to steal out of the room. Faith, I have often formed a resolution to break the ice, and rattle away at any rate; but I don't know how, a single glance from a pair of fine eyes has totally overset my resolution. An impudent fellow may counterfeit modesty, but I'll be hanged if a modest man can ever counterfeit impudence.

HASTINGS. If you could say but half the fine things to them that I have heard you lavish upon the barmaid of an inn, or even a college bed maker . . .

MARLOW. Why, George, I can't say fine things to them—they freeze, they petrify me. They may talk of a comet, or a burning mountain, or some such bagatelle; but to me, a modest woman, drest out in all her finery, is the most tremendous object of the whole creation.

HASTINGS. Ha! Ha! Ha! At this rate, man, how can you ever expect to marry?

MARLOW. Never, unless, as among kings and princes, my bride were to be courted by proxy. If, indeed, like an eastern bridegroom, one were to be introduced to a wife he never saw before, it might be endured; but to go through all the terrors of a formal courtship, together with the episode of aunts, grandmothers and cousins, and at last to blurt out the broad staring question of "Madam, will you marry me?" No, no; that's a strain much above me, I assure you.

HASTINGS. I pity you! But how do you intend behaving to the lady you are come down to visit at the request of your father?

MARLOW. As I behave to all other ladies. Bow very low; answer yes, or no, to all her demands; but for the rest, I don't think I shall venture to look in her face till I see my father's again.

HASTINGS. I'm surprised that one who is so warm a friend can be so cool a lover.

MARLOW. To be explicit, my dear Hastings, my chief inducement down was to be instrumental in forwarding your happiness, not my own. Miss Neville loves you; the family don't know you; as my friend, you are sure of a reception, and let honour do the rest.

HASTINGS. My dear Marlow! But I'll suppress the emotion. Were I a wretch, meanly seeking to carry off a fortune, you should be the last man in the world I would apply to for assistance. But Miss Neville's person is all I ask, and that is mine, both from her deceased father's consent and her own inclination.

MARLOW. Happy man! You have talents and art to captivate any woman. I'm doomed to adore the sex, and yet to converse with the only part of it I despise. This stammer in my address, and this awkward, unprepossessing visage of mine, can never permit me to soar above the reach of a milliner's 'prentice, or one of the duchesses of Drury Lane. Pshaw, this fellow here to interrupt us!

(HARDCASTLE *enters* L)

HARDCASTLE. Gentlemen, once more you are heartily welcome. Which is Mr Marlow?

(MARLOW *advances*)

Sir, you're heartily welcome. It's not my way, you see, to receive my friends with my back to the fire; I like to give them a hearty reception in the old style at my gate: I like to see their horses and trunks taken care of.

MARLOW (*aside*) He has got our names from the servants already. (*To Hardcastle*) We approve your caution and hospitality, sir. (*To Hastings*) I have been thinking, George, of changing our travelling dresses in the morning; I am grown confoundedly ashamed of mine.

(*They cross to* L)

HARDCASTLE. I beg, Mr Marlow, you'll use no ceremony in this house.

HASTINGS. I fancy, Charles, you're right: the first blow is half the battle. I intend opening the campaign with the white and the gold.

HARDCASTLE. Mr Marlow—Mr Hastings—gentlemen—pray be under no restraint in this house. This is Liberty Hall, gentlemen: you may do just as you please here.

MARLOW. Yet, George, if we open the campaign too fiercely at first, we may want ammunition before it is over. I think to reserve the embroidery to secure a retreat.

(*They cross* R)

HARDCASTLE. Your talking of a retreat, Mr Marlow (*he comes between them*), puts me in mind of the Duke of Marlborough, when he went to besiege Denain. He first summoned the garrison . . .

MARLOW. Don't you think the *ventre d'or* waistcoat will do with the plain brown?

HARDCASTLE. He first summoned the garrison, which might consist of about five thousand men . . .

HASTINGS. I think not: brown and yellow mix but very poorly.

HARDCASTLE. I say, gentlemen, as I was telling you, he summoned the garrison, which might consist of about five thousand men . . .

MARLOW. The girls like finery.

HARDCASTLE. Which might consist of about five thousand men, well appointed with stores, ammunition, and other implements of war. "Now," says the Duke of Marlborough, to George Brooks, that stood next to him—you must have heard of George Brooks—"I'll pawn my dukedom," says he, "but I take that garrison without spilling a drop of blood." So . . .

MARLOW. What, my good friend, if you gave us a glass of punch in the meantime, it will help us to carry on the siege with vigour.

HARDCASTLE. Punch, sir! (*Aside*) This is the most unaccountable kind of modesty I ever met with.

MARLOW. Yes, sir, punch. A glass of warm punch after our journey will be comfortable. This is Liberty Hall, you know. (*He sits,* RC)

(DIGGORY *enters* L *with a tankard*)

HARDCASTLE. Here's a cup, sir.

MARLOW (*aside to Hastings*) So, this fellow, in his Liberty Hall, will only let us have just what he pleases.

HARDCASTLE (*taking the cup*) I hope you'll find it to your mind. I have prepared it with my own hands, and I believe you'll own the ingredients are tolerable. Will you be so good as to pledge me, sir? Here, Mr Marlow, here is to our better acquaintance. (*He sits* C, *drinks and gives the cup to Marlow*)

MARLOW (*aside*) A very impudent fellow this; but he's a character, and I'll humour him a little. (*To Hardcastle*) Sir, my service to you. (*He drinks*)

HASTINGS (*aside*) I see this fellow wants to give us his company, and forgets that he's an innkeeper before he has learned to be a gentleman. (*He sits* LC)

MARLOW. From the excellence of your cup, my old friend, I suppose you have a good deal of business in this part of the country. Warm work, now and then, at elections, I suppose. (*He gives the tankard to Hardcastle*)

HARDCASTLE. No, sir, I have long given that work over. Since our betters have hit upon the expedient of electing each other, there's no business for us. (*He gives the tankard to Hastings*)

HASTINGS. So then you have no turn for politics, I find. (*He drinks, then gives the tankard to Marlow*)

HARDCASTLE. Not in the least. There was a time, indeed, I fretted myself about the mistakes of government, like other people; but finding myself every day grow more angry, and the government growing no better, I left it to mend itself. Since that, I no more trouble my head about *Heyder Ally*, or *Ally Cawn*, than about *Ally Croaker*. Sir, my service to you.

HASTINGS. So that with eating above stairs and drinking below, with receiving your friends within, and amusing them without, you lead a good pleasant bustling life of it.

HARDCASTLE. I do stir about a good deal, that's certain. Half the differences of the parish are adjusted in this very parlour.

MARLOW (*after drinking*) And you have an argument in your cup, old gentleman, better than any in Westminster Hall. (*He passes the cup to Hastings*)

HARDCASTLE. Ay, young gentleman, that and a little philosophy.

MARLOW (*aside*) Well, this is the first time I ever heard of an innkeeper's philosophy.

HASTINGS. So then, like an experienced general, you attack them on every quarter. If you find their reason manageable, you attack them with your philosophy; if you find they have no reason, you attack them with this. Here's your health, my philosopher. (*He drinks*)

HARDCASTLE. Good, very good, thank you; ha, ha! Your generalship puts me in mind of Prince Eugene, when he fought the Turks at the battle of Belgrade. You shall hear.

MARLOW. Instead of the battle of Belgrade, I believe it's almost time to talk about supper. What has your philosophy got in the house for supper?

HARDCASTLE. For supper, sir! (*Aside*) Was ever such a request to a man in his own house!

MARLOW. Yes, sir, supper, sir; I begin to feel an appetite. I shall make devilish work tonight in the larder, I promise you. (*He rises*)

HARDCASTLE (*aside*) Such a brazen dog sure never my eyes beheld. (*To Marlow*) Why, really, sir, as for supper, I can't well tell. My Dorothy and the cook maid settle these things between them. I leave these kind of things entirely to them.

---

* Heyder Ally, *Hyder Ali, Sultan of Mysore.*
Ally Cawn, *Ali Khan, Sultan of Bengal.*
Ally Croaker, *an Irish ditty.*

MARLOW. You do, do you?

HARDCASTLE. Entirely. By the bye, I believe tl.ey are in actual consultation upon what's for supper at this moment in the kitchen.

MARLOW. Then I beg they'll admit *me* as one of their privy council. It's a way I have got. When I travel, I always choose to regulate my own supper. Let the cook be called. No offence I hope, sir.

HARDCASTLE. Oh, no, sir, none in the least; yet, I don't know how: our Bridget, the cook maid, is not very communicative upon these occasions. Should we send for her, she might scold us all out of the house.

HASTINGS. Let's see your list of the larder then. I ask it as a favour. I always match my appetite to my bill of fare.

MARLOW (*to* HARDCASTLE, *who looks at them with surprise*) Sir, he's very right, and it's my way too.

HARDCASTLE. Sir, you have a right to command here. Here, Diggory! Roger! Bring us the bill of fare for tonight's supper; I believe it's drawn out. Your manner, Mr Hastings, puts me in mind of my uncle, Colonel Wallop. It was a saying of his, that no man was sure of his supper till he had eaten it.

(ROGER *marches in with the bill of fare, gives it to Marlow and then exits*)

HASTINGS (*aside*) All upon the high ropes! His uncle a colonel! We shall soon hear of his mother being a justice of peace. But let's hear the bill of fare.

MARLOW (*perusing*) What's here? For the first course; for the second course; for the dessert. The devil, sir, do you think we have brought down the whole Joiners Company, or the Corporation of Bedford, to eat up such a supper? Two or three little things, clean and comfortable, will do.

HASTINGS. But let's hear it.

MARLOW (*reading*) For the first course: at the top, a pig and prune sauce.

HASTINGS. Damn your pig, I say.

MARLOW. And damn your prune sauce, I say.

HARDCASTLE. And yet, gentlemen, to men that are hungry pig with prune sauce is very good eating.

MARLOW. At the bottom, a calf's tongue and brains.

HASTINGS. Let your brains be knocked out, my good sir; I don't like them.

MARLOW. Or you may clap them on a plate by themselves. I do.

HARDCASTLE (*aside*) Their impudence confound me. (*To them*) Gentlemen, you are my guests, make what alterations you please. Is there anything else you wish to retrench or alter, gentlemen?

MARLOW. Item. A pork pie, a boiled rabbit and sausages, a

florentine, a shaking pudding, and a dish of tiff—taff—taffety cream?

HASTINGS. Confound your made dishes! I shall be as much at a loss in this house as at a green and yellow dinner at the French Ambassador's table. I'm for plain eating.

HARDCASTLE. I'm sorry, gentlemen, that I have nothing you like; but if there be anything you have a particular fancy to . . .

MARLOW. Why, really, sir, your bill of fare is so exquisite, that any one part of it is full as good as another. Send us what you please. So much for supper. And now to see that our beds are aired, and properly taken care of.

HARDCASTLE. I entreat you'll leave all that to me. You shall not stir a step.

MARLOW. Leave that to you! I protest, sir, you must excuse me; I always look to these things myself.

HARDCASTLE. I must insist, sir, you'll make yourself easy on that head.

MARLOW. You see I'm resolved on it. (*Aside*) A very troublesome fellow as ever I met with.

HARDCASTLE. Well, sir, I'm resolved at least to attend you. (*Aside*) This may be modern modesty, but I never saw anything look so like old-fashioned impudence.

(MARLOW *and* HARDCASTLE *exit* R)

HASTINGS. So I find this fellow's civilities begin to grow troublesome. But who can be angry with those assiduities which are meant to please him? Ha! What do I see? Miss Neville, by all that's happy.

(MISS NEVILLE *enters* L)

MISS NEVILLE. My dear Hastings! To what unexpected good fortune, to what accident, am I to ascribe this happy meeting?

HASTINGS. Rather let me ask the same question, as I could never have hoped to meet my dearest Constance at an inn.

MISS NEVILLE. An inn! Sure you mistake: my aunt, my guardian lives here. What could induce you to think this house an inn?

HASTINGS. My friend Mr Marlow, with whom I came down, and I, have been sent here as to an inn, I assure you. A young fellow, whom we accidentally met at a house hard by, directed us hither.

MISS NEVILLE. Certainly it must be one of my hopeful cousin's tricks, of whom you have heard me talk so often. Ha, ha!

HASTINGS. He whom your aunt intends for you? He of whom I have such just apprehensions?

MISS NEVILLE. You have nothing to fear from him, I assure you. You'd adore him if you knew how heartily he despises me. My aunt knows it too, and has undertaken to court me for him, and actually begins to think she has made a conquest.

HASTINGS. Thou dear dissembler! You must know, my Constance, I have just seized this happy opportunity of my friend's visit here to get admittance into the family. The horses that carried us down are now fatigued with the journey, but they'll soon be refreshed; and then, if my dearest girl will trust in her faithful Hastings, we shall soon be landed in France, where even among slaves the laws of marriage are respected.

Mɪss NEVILLE. I have often told you that, though ready to obey you, I yet should leave my little fortune behind with reluctance. The greatest part of it was left me by my uncle, the India Director, and chiefly consists of jewels. I have been for some time persuading my aunt to let me wear them—I fancy I'm very near succeeding; the instant they are put into my possession, you shall find me ready to make them and myself yours.

HASTINGS. Perish the baubles! Your person is all I desire. In the meantime, my friend Marlow must not be let into his mistake. I know the strange reserve of his temper is such that, if abruptly informed of it, he would instantly quit the house before our plan was ripe for execution.

Mɪss NEVILLE. But how shall we keep him in the deception? Miss Hardcastle is just returned from walking; what if we still continue to deceive him? This, this way . . . (*They move* ʟ *and confer*)

(MARLOW *enters* ʀ)

MARLOW. The assiduities of these good people tease me beyond bearing. My host seems to think it ill manners to leave me alone, and so he claps not only himself but his old-fashioned wife on my back. They talk of coming to sup with us too; and then, I suppose, we are to run the gauntlet through all the rest of the family. What have we got here?

HASTINGS (*moving* ᴄ) My dear Charles, let me congratulate you! The most fortunate accident! Who do you think has just alighted?

MARLOW (*at* ʀ) Cannot guess.

HASTINGS. Our mistresses, boy—Miss Hardcastle and Miss Neville. Give me leave to introduce Miss Constance Neville to your acquaintance. Happening to dine in the neighbourhood, they called on their return to take fresh horses here. Miss Hardcastle has just stepped into the next room, and will be back in an instant. Wasn't it lucky, eh?

MARLOW (*aside*) I have just been mortified enough of all conscience, and here comes something to complete my embarrassment.

HASTINGS. Well, but wasn't it the most fortunate thing in the world!

MARLOW. Oh, yes—very fortunate—a most joyful encounter. But our dresses, George, you know, are in disorder. What if we should postpone the happiness till tomorrow? Tomorrow at her own house—it will be every bit as convenient and rather more respectful. Tomorrow let it be. (*He turns to go*)

Miss Neville (*at* l) By no means, sir. Your ceremony will displease her. The disorder of your dress will show the ardour of your impatience. Besides, she knows you are in the house, and will permit you to see her.

Marlow. Oh, the devil! How shall I support it? Hem! Hem! (*Aside to Hastings*) Hastings, you must not go—you are to assist me, you know. I shall be confoundedly ridiculous. Yet, hang it! I'll take courage. Hem!

Hastings (*aside to Marlow*) Pshaw, man! It's but the first plunge, and all's over. She's but a woman, you know.

Marlow. And of all women, she that I dread most to encounter!

(Miss Hardcastle *enters* l *returning from walking, with a bonnet, &c*)

Hastings (*introducing them*) Miss Hardcastle—Mr Marlow. I'm proud of bringing two persons of such merit together that only want to know, to esteem each other.

Miss Hardcastle (*aside*) Now for meeting my modest gentleman with a demure face, and quite in his own manner. (*After a pause, in which he appears very uneasy and disconcerted*) I'm glad of your safe arrival, sir. I'm told you had some accidents by the way.

Marlow. Only a few, madam. Yes, we had some. Yes, madam, a good many accidents; but should be sorry, madam—or rather, glad—of any accidents that are so agreeably concluded. Hem!

Hastings (*aside to Marlow*) You never spoke better in your whole life. Keep it up, and I'll ensure you the victory.

Miss Hardcastle. I'm afraid you flatter, sir. You that have seen so much of the finest company can find little entertainment in an obscure corner of the country.

Marlow (*gathering courage*) I have lived, indeed, in the world, madam; but I have kept very little company. I have been but an observer upon life, madam, while others were enjoying it.

Miss Neville. But that, I am told, is the way to enjoy it at last.

Hastings (*aside to Marlow*) Cicero never spoke better. Once more, and you are confirmed in assurance for ever.

Marlow (*aside to Hastings*) Hem! Stand by me, then, and when I'm down, throw in a word or two to set me up again.

Miss Hardcastle. An observer, like you, upon life, were, I fear, disagreeably employed, since you must have had much more to censure than to approve.

Marlow. Pardon me, madam: I was always willing to be amused. The folly of most people is rather an object of mirth than uneasiness.

HASTINGS (*aside to Marlow*) Bravo, bravo! Never spoke so well in your whole life. Well, Miss Hardcastle, I see that you and Mr Marlow are going to be very good company. I believe our being here will but embarrass the interview.

MARLOW (*seizing him*) Not in the least, Mr Hastings. We like your company of all things. (*Aside to Hastings*) Zounds, George, sure you won't go? How can you leave us?

HASTINGS. Our presence will but spoil conversation, so we'll retire to the next room. (*Aside to Marlow*) You don't consider, man, that we are to manage a little *tête-à-tête* of our own.

(HASTINGS *and* MISS NEVILLE *exit* R.

MARLOW *hesitates, fetches a chair and sits down, recollects himself and rises in confusion, places a chair for her* LC, *then sits* C)

MISS HARDCASTLE (*after a pause*) But you have not been wholly an observer, I presume, sir. The ladies, I should hope, have employed some part of your addresses. (*She draws her chair towards him*)

MARLOW (*relapsing into timidity*) Pardon me, madam. I—I—I —as yet have studied—only—to—deserve them.

MISS HARDCASTLE. And that, some say, is the very worst way to obtain them.

MARLOW. Perhaps so, madam; but I love to converse only with the more grave and sensible part of the sex. (*He rises*) But I'm afraid I grow tiresome.

MISS HARDCASTLE. Not at all, sir; there is nothing I like so much as grave conversation myself; I could hear it for ever— indeed, I have often been surprised how a man of *sentiment* could ever admire those light airy pleasures, where nothing reaches the heart.

MARLOW (*sitting and moving his chair towards* R) It's—a disease —of the mind, madam. In the variety of tastes, there must be some who, wanting a relish—for—um—a—um . . .

MISS HARDCASTLE. I understand you, sir. There must be some who, wanting a relish for refined pleasures, pretend to despise what they are incapable of tasting. (*She moves towards him*)

MARLOW. My meaning, madam—but infinitely better expressed. And I can't help observing (*sliding his chair away from her*) that in this age of hypocrisy—a . . .

MISS HARDCASTLE (*aside*) Who could ever suppose this fellow impudent upon some occasions! (*To him*) You were going to observe, sir . . .

MARLOW. I was observing, madam—I protest, madam, I forget what I was going to observe.

MISS HARDCASTLE (*aside*) I vow, and so do I. (*To him*) You were observing, sir, that in this age of hypocrisy—something about hypocrisy, sir . . .

MARLOW. Yes, madam; in this age of hypocrisy, there are few who upon strict inquiry, do not—a—a . . .

MISS HARDCASTLE. I understand you perfectly, sir.

MARLOW (*aside*) Egad! And that's more than I do myself.

MISS HARDCASTLE. You mean that, in this hypocritical age, there are few that do not condemn in public what they practise in private, and think they pay every debt to virtue when they praise it.

MARLOW. True, madam, those who have most virtue in their mouths, have least of it in their bosoms. (*He rises*) But I see Miss Neville expecting us in the next room. I would not intrude for the world.

MISS HARDCASTLE. I protest, sir, I never was more agreeably entertained in all my life. Pray go on.

MARLOW. Yes, madam. I was—but she beckons us to join her. Madam, shall I do myself the honour to attend you?

MISS HARDCASTLE. Well, then, I'll follow.

MARLOW (*aside*) This pretty smooth dialogue has done for me.

(MARLOW *bows, then almost runs off* R)

MISS HARDCASTLE. Ha, ha, ha! Was there ever such a sober, sentimental interview? I'm certain he scarce looked in my face the whole time. Yet the fellow, but for his unaccountable bashfulness, is pretty well too: he has good sense, but then so buried in his fears, that it fatigues one more than ignorance. If I could teach him a little confidence it would be doing somebody that I know of a piece of service. But who is that somebody?—that, faith, is a question I can scarcely answer.

(MISS HARDCASTLE *exits* L.

TONY *and* MISS NEVILLE *enter* R, *followed by* MRS HARDCASTLE *and* HASTINGS)

TONY. What do you follow me for, cousin Con? I wonder you're not ashamed to be so very engaging.

MISS NEVILLE. I hope, cousin, one may speak to one's own relations, and not be to blame.

TONY. Ay, but I know what sort of a relation you want to make me, though; but it won't do. I tell you, cousin Con, it won't do, so I beg you'll keep your distance, I want no nearer relationship.

(TONY *moves up stage* C. MISS NEVILLE *follows, coquetting him*)

MRS HARDCASTLE. Well, I vow, Mr Hastings, you are very entertaining. There's nothing in the world I love to talk of so much as London and the fashions, though I was never there myself.

HASTINGS. Never there! You amaze me! From your air and manner, I concluded you had been bred all your life either at Ranelagh, St James's, or Tower Wharf.

MRS HARDCASTLE. O, sir! You're only pleased to say so. We country persons can have no manner at all. I'm in love with the town, and that serves to raise me above some of our neighbouring rustics; but who can have a manner that has never seen the Pantheon, the Grotto Gardens, the Borough, and such places where the nobility chiefly resort? All I can do is to enjoy London at second-hand. I take care to know every *tête-à-tête* from the *Scandalous Magazine*, and have all the fashions as they come out in a letter from the two Miss Rickets of Crooked Lane. Pray, how do you like this head, Mr Hastings?

HASTINGS. Extremely elegant and *degagée*, upon my word, madam. Your *friseur* is a Frenchman, I suppose?

MRS HARDCASTLE. I protest I dressed it myself from a print in the *Ladies Memorandum Book* for the last year.

HASTINGS. Indeed! Such a head in the side box at the play-house would draw as many gazers as my lady mayoress at a city ball.

MRS HARDCASTLE. I vow, since inoculation began, there is no such thing to be seen as a plain woman; so one must dress a little particular, or one may escape in the crowd.

HASTINGS (*bowing*) But that can never be your case, madam, in any dress.

MRS HARDCASTLE. Yet, what signifies *my* dressing, when I have such a piece of antiquity by my side as Mr Hardcastle? All I can say will not argue down a single button from his clothes. I have often wanted him to throw off his great flaxen wig, and where he was bald, to plaster it over like my Lord Pately, with powder.

HASTINGS. You are right, madam; for as among the ladies there are none ugly, so among the men there are none old.

MRS HARDCASTLE. But what do you think his answer was? Why, with his usual *Gothic vivacity, he said I only wanted him to throw off his wig to convert it into a *tête* for my own wearing.

HASTINGS. Intolerable! At your age you may wear what you please, and it must become you.

MRS HARDCASTLE. Pray, Mr Hastings, what do you take to be the most fashionable age about town?

HASTINGS. Some time ago forty was all the mode; but I'm told the ladies intend to bring up fifty for the ensuing winter.

MRS HARDCASTLE. Seriously? Then I shall be too young for the fashion.

HASTINGS. No lady begins now to put on jewels till she's past forty. For instance, Miss there (*indicating Miss Neville*), in a polite circle, would be considered as a child, a mere maker of samplers.

MRS HARDCASTLE. And yet my niece thinks herself as much a woman, and is as fond of jewels, as the oldest of us all.

HASTINGS. Your niece, is she? And the young gentleman, a brother of yours, I should presume?

MRS HARDCASTLE. My son, sir. They are contracted to each

* Gothic, *i.e. rude, barbarous.*

other. Observe their little sports. They fall in and out ten times a day, as if they were man and wife already. (*To Tony and Miss Neville*) Well, Tony, child, what soft things are you saying to your cousin Constance this evening?

TONY (*moving* LC) I have been saying no soft things; but that it's very hard to be followed about so. Ecod! I've not a place in the house that's left to myself but the stable.

MRS HARDCASTLE. Never mind him, Con my dear. He's in another story behind your back.

MISS NEVILLE. There's something generous in my cousin's manner. He falls out before faces to be forgiven in private.

TONY. That's a damned confounded—crack.

MRS HARDCASTLE. Ah, he's a sly one! Don't you think they're like each other about the mouth, Mr Hastings? The Blenkinsop mouth to a T. They're of a size too. Back to back, my pretties, that Mr Hastings may see you. Come, Tony.

TONY. You had as good not make me, I tell you. (*Measuring, he knocks his head against hers*)

MISS NEVILLE (*moving* L) O lud! He has almost cracked my head.

MRS HARDCASTLE. O, the monster! For shame, Tony. You a man, and behave so!

TONY. If I'm a man, let me have my fortin. Ecod, I'll not be made a fool of any longer.

MRS HARDCASTLE. Is this, ungrateful boy, all that I'm to get for the pains I have taken in your education? I, that have rocked you in your cradle, and fed that pretty mouth with a spoon! Did not I work that waistcoat to make you genteel? Did not I prescribe for you, every day, and weep while the receipt was operating?

TONY. Ecod! You had reason to weep, for you have been dosing me ever since I was born. I have gone through every receipt in *The Complete Housewife* ten times over; and you have thoughts of coursing me through *Quincy next spring. But, ecod! I tell you, I'll not be made a fool of no longer.

MRS HARDCASTLE. Wasn't it all for your good, viper? Wasn't it all for your good?

TONY. I wish you'd let me and my good alone, then. Snubbing this way when I'm in spirits. If I'm to have any good, let it come of itself; not to keep dinging it, dinging it into one so.

MRS HARDCASTLE. That's false; I never see you when you're in spirits. No, Tony, you then go to the alehouse or kennel. I'm never to be delighted with your agreeable wild notes, unfeeling monster!

TONY. Ecod, mamma, your own notes are the wildest of the two.

MRS HARDCASTLE. Was ever the like? But I see he wants to break my heart, I see he does.

* Quincy, *the compiler of a "Complete English Dispensatory ".*

HASTINGS. Dear madam, permit me to lecture the young gentleman a little. I'm certain I can persuade him to his duty.

MRS HARDCASTLE. Well, I must retire. Come, Constance, my love. You see, Mr Hastings, the wretchedness of my situation. Was ever poor woman so plagued with a dear, sweet, pretty, provoking undutiful boy?

(MRS HARDCASTLE *and* MISS NEVILLE *exit* R)

TONY (*singing*)

> There was a young man riding by,
> And fain would have his will.
> Rang do didlo dee.

Don't mind her. Let her cry. It's the comfort of her heart. I have seen her and sister cry over a book for an hour together, and they said they liked the book the better the more it made them cry.

HASTINGS. Then you're no friend to the ladies I find, my pretty young gentleman?

TONY. That's as I find 'um.

HASTINGS. Not to her of your mother's choosing, I dare answer! And yet she appears to me a pretty well-tempered girl.

TONY. That's because you don't know her as well as I. Ecod! I know every inch about her; and there's not a more bitter, cantankerous toad in all Christendom.

HASTINGS (*aside*) Pretty encouragement this for a lover.

TONY. I have seen her since the height of that. She has as many tricks as a hare in a thicket, or a colt the first day's breaking.

HASTINGS. To me she appears sensible and silent.

TONY. Ay, before company; but when she's with her playmates, she's as loud as a hog in a gate.

HASTINGS. But there is a meek modesty about her that charms me.

TONY. Yes, but curb her never so little, she kicks up, and you're flung in the ditch.

HASTINGS. Well, but you must allow her a little beauty—yes, you must allow her some beauty.

TONY. Bandbox! She's all a made-up thing, mun. Ah, could you but see Bet Bouncer of these parts, you might then talk of beauty! Ecod, she has two eyes as black as sloes, and cheeks as broad and red as a pulpit cushion. She'd make two of she.

HASTINGS. Well, what say you to a friend that would take this bitter bargain off your hands?

TONY. Anon.

HASTINGS. Would you thank him that would take Miss Neville, and leave you to happiness and your dear Betsy?

TONY. Ay; but where is there such a friend, for who would take *her*?

HASTINGS. I am he. If you but assist me, I'll engage to whip her off to France, and you shall never hear more of her.

TONY. Assist you! Ecod I will, to the last drop of my blood. I'll clap a pair of horses to your chaise that shall trundle you off in a twinkling, and may be get you a part of her fortin beside in jewels, that you little dream of.

HASTINGS. My dear 'squire, this looks like a lad of spirit.

TONY. Come along then, and you shall see more of my spirit before you have done with me. (*He sings*)

> We are the boys
> That fears no noise,
> Where thundering cannons roar.

(*Exeunt,* L)

CURTAIN

ACT III

As the CURTAIN *rises*, HARDCASTLE *enters* R.

HARDCASTLE. What could my old friend Sir Charles mean by recommending his son as the modestest young man in town? To me he appears the most impudent piece of brass that ever spoke with a tongue. He has taken possession of the easy chair by the fireside already. He took off his boots in the parlour, and desired me to see them taken care of. I'm desirous to know how his impudence affects my daughter—she will certainly be shocked at it.

(MISS HARDCASTLE *enters* L, *plainly dressed*)

Well, my Kate, I see you have changed your dress as I bid you; and yet I believe there was no great occasion.

MISS HARDCASTLE. I find such a pleasure, sir, in obeying your commands, that I take care to observe them without ever debating their propriety.

HARDCASTLE. And yet, Kate, I sometimes give you some cause, particularly when I recommended my *modest* gentleman to you as a lover today.

MISS HARDCASTLE. You taught me to expect something extraordinary, and I find the original exceeds the description.

HARDCASTLE. I was never so surprised in my life! He has quite confounded all my faculties.

MISS HARDCASTLE. I never saw anything like it: and a man of the world too!

HARDCASTLE. Ay, he learned it all abroad—what a fool was I, to think a young man could learn modesty by travelling. He might as soon learn wit at a masquerade.

MISS HARDCASTLE. It seems all natural to him.

HARDCASTLE. A good deal assisted by bad company and a French dancing-master.

MISS HARDCASTLE. Sure, you mistake, papa: a French dancing-master could never have taught him that timid look—that awkward address—that bashful manner . . .

HARDCASTLE. Whose look, whose manner, child?

MISS HARDCASTLE. Mr Marlow's: his *mauvaise honte*, his timidity struck me at the first sight.

HARDCASTLE. Then your first sight deceived you; for I think him one of the most brazen first sights that ever astonished my senses.

MISS HARDCASTLE. Sure, sir, you rally! I never saw any one so modest.

HARDCASTLE. And can you be serious! I never saw such a bouncing, swaggering puppy since I was born. Bully Dawson was but a fool to him.

MISS HARDCASTLE. Surprising! He met me with a respectful bow, a stammering voice, and a look fixed on the ground.

HARDCASTLE. He met me with a loud voice, a lordly air, and a familiarity that made my blood freeze again.

MISS HARDCASTLE. He treated me with diffidence and respect; censured the manners of the age; admired the prudence of girls that never laughed; tired me with apologies for being tiresome, then left the room with a bow, and (*she mimics Marlow*) "Madam, I would not for the world detain you."

HARDCASTLE. He spoke to me as if he knew me all his life before. Asked twenty questions, and never waited for an answer. Interrupted my best remarks with some silly pun; and when I was in my best story of the Duke of Marlborough and Prince Eugene, he asked me if I had not a good hand at making punch. Yes, Kate, he asked your father if he was a maker of punch!

MISS HARDCASTLE. One of us must certainly be mistaken.

HARDCASTLE. If he be what he has shown himself, I'm determined he shall never have my consent.

MISS HARDCASTLE. And if he be the sullen thing I take him, he shall never have mine.

HARDCASTLE. In one thing then we are agreed—to reject him.

MISS HARDCASTLE. Yes, but upon conditions. For if you should find him less impudent, and I more presuming; if you find him more respectful, and I more importunate . . . I don't know—the fellow is well enough for a man. Certainly we don't meet many such at a horse race in the country.

HARDCASTLE. If we should find him so—but that's impossible. The first appearance has done my business. I'm seldom deceived in that.

MISS HARDCASTLE. And yet there may be many good qualities under that first appearance.

HARDCASTLE. Ay, when a girl finds a fellow's outside to her taste, she then sets about guessing the rest of his furniture. With her, a smooth face stands for good sense, and a genteel figure for every virtue.

MISS HARDCASTLE. I hope, sir, a conversation begun with a compliment to my good sense won't end with a sneer at my understanding?

HARDCASTLE. Pardon me, Kate. But if young Mr Brazen can find the art of reconciling contradictions, he may please us both perhaps.

MISS HARDCASTLE. And as one of us must be mistaken, what if we go to make further discoveries?

HARDCASTLE. Agreed; but depend on't I'm in the right.

MISS HARDCASTLE. And depend on't I'm not much in the wrong.

(HARDCASTLE *and* MISS HARDCASTLE *exit* L.
TONY *runs in* R *with a casket*)

TONY. Ecod, I have got them. Here they are. My cousin Con's necklaces, bobs and all. My mother shan't cheat the poor souls out of their fortin neither. Oh, my genus, is that you?

(HASTINGS *enters* L)

HASTINGS. My dear friend, how have you managed with your mother? I hope you have amused her with pretending love for your cousin, and that you are willing to be reconciled at last? Our horses will be refreshed in a short time, and we shall soon be ready to set off.

TONY. And here's something to bear your charges by the way. (*He gives Hastings the casket*) Your sweetheart's jewels. Keep them, and hang those I say that would rob you of one of them.

HASTINGS. But how have you procured them from your mother?

TONY. Ask me no questions, and I'll tell you no fibs; I procured them by the rule of thumb. If I had not a key to every drawer in mother's bureau, how could I go to the alehouse so often as I do? An honest man may rob himself of his own at any time.

HASTINGS. Thousands do it every day. But, to be plain with you, Miss Neville is endeavouring to procure them from her aunt this very instant. If she succeeds, it will be the most delicate way at least of obtaining them.

TONY. Well, keep them till you know how it will be. But I know how it will be well enough; she'd as soon part with the only sound tooth in her head.

HASTINGS. But I dread the effects of her resentment when she finds she has lost them.

TONY. Never you mind her resentment—leave *me* to manage that. I don't value her resentment the bounce of a cracker. Zounds, here they are! *Morrice, prance!

(HASTINGS *exits* L.
MRS HARDCASTLE *and* MISS NEVILLE *enter* R)

MRS HARDCASTLE. Indeed, Constance, you amaze me. Such a girl as you want jewels. It will be time enough for jewels, my dear, twenty years hence, when your beauty begins to want repairs.

MISS NEVILLE. But what will repair beauty at forty will certainly improve it at twenty, madam.

MRS HARDCASTLE. Yours, my dear, can admit of none. That

---

* Morrice, prance!, *i.e. off you trot: connected with morris-dance.*

natural blush is beyond a thousand ornaments. Besides, child, jewels are quite out at present. Don't you see half the ladies of our acquaintance—my Lady Kill-daylight, and Mrs Crump, and the rest of them, carry their jewels to Town, and bring nothing but paste and marcasites back?

MISS NEVILLE. But who knows, madam, but somebody that shall be nameless would like me best with all my little finery about me?

MRS HARDCASTLE. Consult your glass, my dear, and then see if with such a pair of eyes you want any better sparklers. What do you think, Tony, my dear—does your cousin Con want any jewels, in your eyes, to set off her beauty?

TONY. That's as hereafter may be.

MISS NEVILLE. My dear aunt, if you knew how it would oblige me.

MRS HARDCASTLE. A parcel of old-fashioned rose and table-cut things. They would make you look like the court of King Solomon at a puppet-show. Besides, I believe I can't readily come at them; they may be missing, for aught I know to the contrary.

TONY (aside to Mrs Hardcastle) Then why don't you tell her so at once, as she's so longing for them. Tell her they're lost. It's the only way to quiet her. Say they're lost, and call me to bear witness.

MRS HARDCASTLE (aside to Tony) You know, my dear, I'm only keeping them for you. So if I say they're gone, you'll bear me witness, will you? He! He! He!

TONY (aside to Mrs Hardcastle) Never fear me. Ecod, I'll say I saw them taken out with my own eyes.

MISS NEVILLE. I desire them but for a day, madam; just to be permitted to show them as relics, and then they may be locked up again.

MRS HARDCASTLE. To be plain with you, my dear Constance, if I could find them, you should have them. They're missing, I assure you. Lost, for aught I know; but we must have patience, wherever they are.

MISS NEVILLE. I'll not believe it. This is but a shallow pretence to deny me. I know they're too valuable to be so slightly kept, and as you are to answer for the loss.

MRS HARDCASTLE. Don't be alarmed, Constance. If they be lost, I must restore an equivalent. But my son knows they are missing, and not to be found.

TONY. That I can bear witness to. They are missing, and not to be found—I'll take my oath on't.

MRS HARDCASTLE. You must learn resignation, my dear; for though we lose our fortune, yet we should not lose our patience. See me, how calm I am.

MISS NEVILLE. Ay, people are generally calm at the misfortune of others.

Mrs Hardcastle. Now, I wonder a girl of your good sense should waste a thought upon such trumpery. We shall soon find them; and in the meantime you shall make use of my garnets till your jewels be found.

Miss Neville. I detest garnets.

Mrs Hardcastle. The most becoming things in the world to set off a clear complexion. You have often seen how well they look upon me. You *shall* have them.

(Mrs Hardcastle *exits* r)

Miss Neville. I dislike them of all things. You shan't stir. Was ever anything so provoking—to mislay my own jewels, and force me to wear trumpery.

Tony. Don't be a fool. If she gives you the garnets, take what you can get. The jewels are your own already. I have stolen them out of her bureau, and she does not know it. Fly to your spark, he'll tell you more of the matter. Leave me to manage her.

Miss Neville. My dear cousin!

Tony. Vanish!

(Miss Neville *exits* l)

She's here, and has missed them already. Zounds! how she fidgets and spits about like a Catherine wheel.

(Mrs Hardcastle *enters* r)

Mrs Hardcastle. Confusion! Thieves! Robbers! We are cheated, plundered, broke open, undone.

Tony. What's the matter, what's the matter, mamma? I hope nothing has happened to any of the good family.

Mrs Hardcastle. We are robbed. My bureau has been broken open, the jewels taken out, and I'm undone.

Tony. Oh! is that all? Ha! Ha! Ha! By the laws, I never saw it better acted in my life. Ecod, I thought you were ruined in earnest. Ha! Ha! Ha!

Mrs Hardcastle. Why, boy, I *am* ruined in earnest. My bureau has been broken open, and all taken away.

Tony. Stick to that; ha! ha! stick to that. I'll bear witness you know, call me to bear witness.

Mrs Hardcastle. I tell you, Tony, by all that's precious, the jewels are gone, and I shall be ruined for ever.

Tony. Sure I know they're gone, and I am to say so.

Mrs Hardcastle. My dearest Tony, but hear me. They're gone, I say.

Tony. By the laws, mamma, you make me for to laugh. Ha! Ha! I know who took them well enough. Ha! Ha! Ha!

Mrs Hardcastle. Was there ever such a blockhead, that can't tell the difference between jest and earnest. I tell you I'm not in jest, booby.

Tony. That's right, that's right: you must be in a bitter passion, and then nobody will suspect either of us. I'll bear witness that they are gone.

Mrs Hardcastle. Was there ever such a cross-grained brute, that won't hear me? Can you bear witness that you're no better than a fool? Was ever poor woman so beset with fools on one hand and thieves on the other.

Tony. I can bear witness to that.

Mrs Hardcastle. Bear witness again, you blockhead you, and I'll turn you out of the room directly. My poor niece, what will become of *her*! Do you laugh, you unfeeling brute, as if you enjoyed my distress?

Tony. I can bear witness to that.

Mrs Hardcastle. Do you insult me, monster? I'll teach you to vex your mother, I will.

Tony. I can bear witness to that.

(Tony *runs off* l. Mrs Hardcastle *runs after him.*
Miss Hardcastle *and a* Maid *enter* r)

Miss Hardcastle. What an unaccountable creature is that brother of mine, to send them to the house as an inn. Ha! Ha! I don't wonder at his impudence.

Maid. But what is more, madam, the young gentleman, as you passed by in your present dress, asked me if you were the bar-maid. He mistook you for the barmaid, madam.

Miss Hardcastle. Did he? Then, as I live, I'm resolved to keep up the delusion. Tell me, Pimple, how do you like my pre-sent dress? Don't you think I look something like Cherry in the *Beaux' Stratagem*?

Maid. It's the dress, madam, that every lady wears in the country, but when she visits or receives company.

Miss Hardcastle. And are you sure he does not remember my face or person?

Maid. Certain of it.

Miss Hardcastle. I vow I thought so; for though we spoke for some time together, yet his fears were such that he never once looked up during the interview. Indeed, if he had, my bonnet would have kept him from seeing me.

Maid. But what do you hope from keeping him in his mistake?

Miss Hardcastle. In the first place, I shall be *seen*, and that is no small advantage to a girl who brings her face to market. Then I shall perhaps make an acquaintance, and that's no small victory gained over one who never addresses any but the wildest of her sex. But my chief aim is to take my gentleman off his guard, and like an invisible champion of romance examine the giant's force before I offer to combat.

Maid. But are you sure you can act your part and disguise

your voice, so that he may mistake that, as he has already mistaken your person?

MISS HARDCASTLE. Never fear me. I think I have got the true bar cant: Did your honour call?—Attend the *Lion there—Pipes and tobacco for the Angel—the Lamb has been outrageous this half hour.

MAID. It will do, madam, but he's here.

(*The* MAID *exits* R.
MARLOW *enters* L)

MARLOW. What a bawling in every part of the house; I have scarce a moment's repose. If I go to the best room, there I find my host and his story. If I fly to the gallery, there we have my hostess, with her curtsy down to the ground. I have at last got a moment to myself, and now for recollection. (*He walks about and muses*)

MISS HARDCASTLE. Did you call, sir? Did your honour call?

MARLOW (*crossing* R) As for Miss Hardcastle, she's too grave and sentimental for me.

MISS HARDCASTLE. Did your honour call? (*She places herself before him*)

MARLOW. No, child. (*He crosses* L) Besides, from the glimpse I had of her, I think she squints.

MISS HARDCASTLE. I'm sure, sir, I heard the bell ring.

MARLOW. No, no. (*Musing*) I have pleased my father, however, by coming down, and I'll tomorrow please myself by returning.

MISS HARDCASTLE. Perhaps the other gentleman called, sir?

MARLOW. I tell you, no.

MISS HARDCASTLE. I should be glad to know, sir. We have such a parcel of servants.

MARLOW. No, no, I tell you. (*He looks full in her face*) Yes, child, I think I did call. I wanted—I wanted—I vow, child, you are vastly handsome.

MISS HARDCASTLE (*at* RC) O la, sir! you'll make one ashamed.

MARLOW (*at* LC) Never saw a more sprightly malicious eye. Yes, yes, my dear, I did call. Have you got any of your—a—what d'ye call it, in the house?

MISS HARDCASTLE. No, sir; we have been out of that these ten days.

MARLOW. One may call in this house, I find, to very little purpose. Suppose I should call for a taste, just by way of trial, of the nectar of your lips; perhaps I might be disappointed in that too?

MISS HARDCASTLE. Nectar! Nectar! that's a liquor there's no call for in these parts. French, I suppose. We keep no French wines here, sir.

---

* Lion, Angel, Lamb, *the names of rooms in the tavern.*

MARLOW. Of true English growth, I assure you.

MISS HARDCASTLE. Then it's odd I should not know it. We brew all sorts of wines in this house, and I have lived here these eighteen years.

MARLOW. Eighteen years! Why one would think, child, you kept the bar before you were born. How old are you?

MISS HARDCASTLE. O, sir! I must not tell my age. They say women and music should never be dated.

MARLOW. To guess at this distance, you can't be much above forty. (He approaches her) Yet nearer, I don't think so much. (He approaches nearer) By coming close to some women they look younger still: but when we come very close indeed . . . (He attempts to kiss her)

MISS HARDCASTLE. Pray, sir, keep your distance. One would think you wanted to know one's age as they do horses, by mark of mouth.

MARLOW. I protest, child, you use me extremely ill. If you keep me at this distance, how is it possible you and I can ever be acquainted?

MISS HARDCASTLE. And who wants to be acquainted with you? I want no such acquaintance, not I. I'm sure you did not treat Miss Hardcastle, that was here awhile ago, in this obstropolous manner. I'll warrant me, before her you looked dashed, and kept bowing to the ground, and talked for all the world as if you was before a justice of peace.

MARLOW (aside) Egad! she has hit it sure enough. (To her) In awe of her, child? Ha, ha, ha! A mere awkward, squinting thing. No, no; I find you don't know me. I laughed and rallied her a little; but I was unwilling to be too severe: no, I could not be too severe, curse me! (He crosses R)

MISS HARDCASTLE. O, then, sir, you are a favourite, I find, among the ladies?

MARLOW. Yes, my dear, a great favourite. And yet, hang me, I don't see what they find in me to follow. At the Ladies Club in town I'm called their agreeable Rattle. Rattle, child, is not my real name, but one I'm known by. My name is Solomons. Mr Solomons, my dear, at your service. (He attempts to kiss her)

MISS HARDCASTLE. Hold, sir; you were introducing me to your club, not to yourself. And you're so great a favourite there, you say?

MARLOW. Yes, my dear. There's Mrs Mantrap, Lady Betty Blackleg, the Countess of Slingo, Mrs Longhorns, old Miss Biddy Buckskin, and your humble servant, keep up the spirit of the place. (He crosses L)

MISS HARDCASTLE. Then it's a very merry place, I suppose?

MARLOW. Yes, as merry as cards, supper, wine and old women can make us.

MISS HARDCASTLE. And their agreeable Rattle, ha, ha, ha!

MARLOW (*aside*) Egad, I don't quite like this chit; she looks knowing, methinks. (*To her*) You laugh, child!

MISS HARDCASTLE. I can't but laugh to think what time they all have for minding their work or their family.

MARLOW (*aside*) All's well, she don't laugh at me. (*To her*) Do you ever work, child?

MISS HARDCASTLE. Ay, sure; there's not a screen or a quilt in the whole house but can bear witness to that.

MARLOW. Odso! Then you must show me your embroidery. I embroider and draw patterns myself a little. If you want a judge of your work, you must apply to me. (*He seizes her hand*)

MISS HARDCASTLE. Ay, but the colours don't look well by candle-light. You shall see all in the morning. (*She struggles*)

(HARDCASTLE *enters and stands in surprise*)

MARLOW. And why not now, my angel? Such beauty fires beyond the power of resistance. Pshaw! The father here! My old luck: * I never nicked seven, that I did not throw ames-ace three times following.

(MARLOW *exits* L)

HARDCASTLE. So, madam. So I find *this* is your *modest* lover—this is your humble admirer, that kept his eyes fixed on the ground and only adored at humble distance. Kate, Kate, art thou not ashamed to deceive your father so?

MISS HARDCASTLE. Never trust me, my dear papa, but he's still the modest man I first took him for; you'll be convinced of it as well as I.

HARDCASTLE. By the hand of my body, I believe, his impudence is infectious! Didn't I see him seize your hand? Didn't I see him haul you about like a milk-maid? And now you talk of his respect, and his modesty, forsooth!

MISS HARDCASTLE. But if I shortly convince you of his modesty, that he has only the faults that will pass off with time, and the virtues that will improve with age, I hope you'll forgive him.

HARDCASTLE. The girl would actually make one run mad! I tell you I'll not be convinced—I am convinced. He has scarcely been three hours in the house, and he has already encroached on all my prerogatives. You may like his impudence, and call it modesty; but my son-in-law, madam, must have very different qualifications.

MISS HARDCASTLE. Sir, I ask but this night to convince you.

HARDCASTLE. You shall not have half the time, for I have thoughts of turning him out this very hour.

MISS HARDCASTLE. Give me that hour then, and I hope to satisfy you.

* I never nicked seven . . . *To nick seven is to hazard one's money on seven. Consequently to throw "ames-ace"* (= *ambs-ace, two aces together*) *would be very bad luck.*

HARDCASTLE. Well, an hour let it be then. But I'll have no trifling with your father. All fair and open, do you mind me?

MISS HARDCASTLE. I hope, sir, you have ever found that I considered your commands as my pride; for your kindness is such that my duty as yet has been inclination.

They exit as—

the CURTAIN *falls*

ACT IV

SCENE—*The same.*

When the CURTAIN *rises,* HASTINGS *and* MISS NEVILLE *enter* L.

HASTINGS. You surprise me! Sir Charles Marlow expected here this night? Where have you had your information?

MISS NEVILLE. You may depend upon it. I just saw his letter to Mr Hardcastle, in which he tells him he intends setting out a few hours after his son.

HASTINGS. Then, my Constance, all must be completed before he arrives. He knows me; and should he find me here would discover my name, and perhaps my designs, to the rest of the family.

MISS NEVILLE. The jewels I hope are safe.

HASTINGS. Yes, yes. I have sent them to Marlow, who keeps the keys of our baggage. In the meantime I'll go to prepare matters for our elopement. I have had the 'squire's promise of a fresh pair of horses; and, if I should not see him again, will write him further directions.

MISS NEVILLE. Well, success attend you! In the meantime, I'll go amuse my aunt with the old pretence of a violent passion for my cousin.

(*They exit* L.
MARLOW *enters* R, *followed by a* SERVANT)

MARLOW. I wonder what Hastings could mean by sending me so valuable a thing as a casket to keep for him, when he knows the only place I have is the seat of a post-coach at an inn-door. Have you deposited the casket with the landlady, as I ordered you? Have you put it into her own hands?

SERVANT. Yes, your honour.

MARLOW. She said she'd keep it safe, did she?

SERVANT. Yes, she said she'd keep it safe enough; she asked me how I came by it, and she said she had a great mind to make me give an account of myself.

(*The* SERVANT *exits* L)

MARLOW. Ha, ha, ha! They're safe, however. What an unaccountable set of beings have we got amongst! This little barmaid, though, runs in my head most strangely, and drives out the absurdities of all the rest of the family. She's mine, she must be mine, or I'm greatly mistaken.

(HASTINGS *enters* L)

HASTINGS. Bless me! I quite forgot to tell her that I intended to prepare at the bottom of the garden. Marlow here, and in spirits too!

MARLOW. Give me joy, George! Crown me, shadow me with laurels! Well, George, after all, we modest fellows don't want for success among the women.

HASTINGS. Some women, you mean. But what success has your honour's modesty been crowned with now, that it grows so insolent upon us?

MARLOW. Didn't you see the tempting, brisk, lovely little thing that runs about the house with a bunch of keys to its girdle?

HASTINGS. Well, and what then?

MARLOW. She's mine, you rogue you. Such fire, such motion, such eyes, such lips—but, egad, she would not let me kiss them though.

HASTINGS. But are you so sure, so very sure of her?

MARLOW. Why, man, she talked of showing me her work above stairs, and I'm to improve the pattern.

HASTINGS. But how can you, Charles, go about to rob a woman of her honour?

MARLOW. Pshaw, pshaw! I don't intend to rob her, take my word for it; there's nothing in this house I shan't honestly pay for.

HASTINGS. I believe the girl has virtue.

MARLOW. And if she has, I should be the last man in the world that would attempt to corrupt it.

HASTINGS. You have taken care, I hope, of the casket I sent you to lock up? It's in safety?

MARLOW. Yes, yes, it's safe enough. I have taken care of it. But how could you think the seat of a post-coach at an inn-door a place of safety? Ah, numskull! I have taken better precautions for you than you did for yourself—I have . . .

HASTINGS. What?

MARLOW. I have sent it to the landlady to keep for you.

HASTINGS. To the landlady?

MARLOW. The landlady.

HASTINGS. You did?

MARLOW. I did. She's to be answerable for its forthcoming, you know.

HASTINGS. Yes, she'll bring it forth with a witness.

MARLOW. Wasn't I right? I believe you'll allow that I acted prudently upon this occasion.

HASTINGS (aside) He must not see my uneasiness.

MARLOW. You seem a little disconcerted though, methinks. Sure nothing has happened?

HASTINGS. No, nothing. Never was in better spirits in all my life. And so you left it with the landlady, who, no doubt, very readily undertook the charge?

MARLOW. Rather too readily; for she not only kept the casket,

but, through her great precaution, was going to keep the mes-
senger too. Ha, ha, ha!

HASTINGS. He, he, he! They're safe, however.

MARLOW. As a guinea in a miser's purse.

HASTINGS (*aside*) So now all hopes of fortune are at an end,
and we must set off without it. (*To Marlow*) Well, Charles, I'll
leave you to your meditations on the pretty barmaid, and, ha, ha,
ha! May you be as successful for yourself as you have been for me.

(HASTINGS *exits* L)

MARLOW. Thank ye, George. I ask no more. Ha, ha, ha!

(HARDCASTLE *enters* R)

HARDCASTLE. I no longer know my own house. It's turned all
topsy-turvy. His servants have got drunk already. I'll bear it no
longer; and yet from my respect for his father, I'll be calm. (*To
Marlow; bowing low*) Mr Marlow, your servant, I'm your very
humble servant.

MARLOW. Sir, your humble servant. (*Aside*) What's to be the
wonder now?

HARDCASTLE. I believe, sir, you must be sensible, sir, that no
man alive ought to be more welcome than your father's son, sir.
I hope you think so?

MARLOW. I do, from my soul, sir. I don't want much entreaty.
I generally make my father's son welcome wherever he goes.

HARDCASTLE. I believe you do, from my soul, sir. But though
I say nothing to your own conduct, that of your servants is insuff-
erable. Their manner of drinking is setting a very bad example
in this house, I assure you.

MARLOW. I protest, my very good sir, that's no fault of mine.
If they don't drink as they ought, *they* are to blame: I ordered
them not to spare the cellar; I did, I assure you. (*He calls* L) Here,
let one of my servants come up. (*To Hardcastle*) My positive directions were, that as I did not drink myself, they should make up
for my deficiencies below.

HARDCASTLE. Then they had your orders for what they do?
I'm satisfied.

MARLOW. They had, I assure you: you shall hear from one of
themselves.

(JEREMY *enters* L, *drunk*)

You, Jeremy! Come forward, sirrah! What were my orders? Were
you not told to drink freely, and call for what you thought fit, for
the good of the house?

HARDCASTLE (*aside*) I begin to lose my patience.

JEREMY. Please, your honour, liberty and Fleet Street for ever!
Though I'm but a servant, I'm as good as another man: I'll drink
for no man before supper, sir, damme! Good liquor will sit upon

a good supper, but a good supper will not sit upon—(*hiccup*)—upon my conscience, sir.

(JEREMY *exits* L)

MARLOW. You see, my old friend, the fellow is as drunk as he can possibly be. I don't know what you'd have more, unless you'd have the poor devil soused in a beer barrel.

HARDCASTLE (*aside*) Zounds! he'll drive me distracted if I contain myself any longer. Mr Marlow, sir, I have submitted to your insolence for more than four hours, and I see no likelihood of its coming to an end. I'm now resolved to be master here, sir, and I desire that you and your drunken pack may leave my house directly.

MARLOW. Leave your house! Sure you jest, my good friend! What, when I'm doing what I can to please you?

HARDCASTLE. I tell you, sir, you don't please me; so I desire you'll leave my house.

MARLOW. Sure you cannot be serious. At this time o'night, and such a night! You only mean to banter me.

HARDCASTLE. I tell you, sir, I'm serious; and now that my passions are roused, I say this house is mine, sir; this house is mine, and I command you to leave it directly.

MARLOW. Ha, ha, ha! A puddle in a storm. I shan't stir a step, I assure you. (*In a serious tone*) This your house, fellow! It's my house; this is my house—mine while I choose to stay. What right have you to bid me leave this house, sir? I never met with such impudence, curse me, never in my whole life before. (*He crosses* R)

HARDCASTLE. Nor I, confound me if ever I did. To come to my house, to call for what he likes, to turn me out of my own chair, to insult the family, to order his servants to get drunk, and then to tell me, "This house is mine, sir"! By all that's impudent, it makes me laugh. Ha, ha, ha, ha! Pray, sir (*bantering*), as you take the house, what think you of taking the rest of the furniture? There's a pair of silver candlesticks, and there's a fire-screen, and here's a pair of brazen-nosed bellows; perhaps you may take a fancy to them?

MARLOW. Bring me your bill, sir, bring me your bill, and let's make no more words about it.

HARDCASTLE. There are a set of prints too. What think you of *The Rake's Progress* for your own apartment?

MARLOW. Bring me your bill, I say; and I'll leave you and your infernal house directly. (*He crosses* L)

HARDCASTLE. Then there's a mahogany table, that you may see your own face in.

MARLOW. My bill, I say.

HARDCASTLE. I had forgot the great chair, for your own particular slumbers, after a hearty meal.

MARLOW. Zounds! Bring me my bill I say, and let's hear no more on't.

HARDCASTLE. Young man, young man, from your father's letter to me, I was taught to expect a well-bred, modest man as a visitor here; but now I find him no better than a coxcomb and a bully; but he will be down here presently and shall hear more of it.

(HARDCASTLE *exits* R)

MARLOW. How's this? Sure I have not mistaken the house! Everything looks like an inn. The servants cry, "Coming". The attendance is awkward; the barmaid, too, to attend us. But she's here, and will further inform me. Whither so fast, child? A word with you.

(MISS HARDCASTLE *enters* R, *crossing to* L)

MISS HARDCASTLE. Let it be short then, I'm in a hurry. (*Aside*) I believe he begins to find out his mistake, but it's too soon quite to undeceive him.

MARLOW. Pray, child, answer me one question. What are you, and what may your business in this house be?

MISS HARDCASTLE. A relation of the family, sir.

MARLOW. What, a poor relation?

MISS HARDCASTLE. Yes, sir. A poor relation appointed to keep the keys, and to see that the guests want nothing in my power to give them.

MARLOW. That is, you act as the barmaid of this inn.

MISS HARDCASTLE. Inn! O la! What brought that in your head? One of the best families in the county keep an inn! Ha, ha, ha! Old Mr Hardcastle's house an inn!

MARLOW. Mr Hardcastle's house! Is this house Mr Hardcastle's house, child?

MISS HARDCASTLE. Ay, sure. Whose else should it be?

MARLOW. So then all's out, and I have been damnably imposed on. Oh confound my stupid head. I shall be laughed at over the whole town. I shall be stuck up in *caricatura* in all the print shops—*The Dullissimo *Maccaroni*. To mistake this house of all others for an inn and my father's old friend for an innkeeper! What a swaggering puppy must he take me for. What a silly puppy do I find myself. There again, may I be hanged, my dear, but I mistook you for the barmaid.

MISS HARDCASTLE. Dear me, dear me! I'm sure there's nothing in my behaviour (*half crying*) to put me upon a level with one of that stamp.

MARLOW. Nothing, my dear, nothing; but I was in for a list of blunders, and could not help making you a subscriber. My stupidity saw everything the wrong way. I mistook your assiduity

* Maccaroni, *i.e. fop.*

for assurance, and your simplicity for allurement. But it's over—
this house I no more show *my* face in.

MISS HARDCASTLE. I hope, sir, I have done nothing to dis-
oblige you. I'm sure I should be sorry to affront any gentleman
who has been so polite, and said so many civil things to me. I'm
sure I should be sorry—(*pretending to cry*) if he left the family upon
my account. I'm sure I should be sorry if people said anything
amiss, since I have no fortune but my character.

MARLOW (*aside*) By heaven, she weeps! This is the first mark
of tenderness I ever had from a modest woman, and it touches
me. (*To her*) Excuse me, my lovely girl, you are the only part of
the family I leave with reluctance. But to be plain with you, the
difference of our birth, fortune and education make an honour-
able connexion impossible; and I can never harbour a thought of
betraying simplicity that trusted in my honour, or bringing ruin
upon one whose only fault was being too lovely.

MISS HARDCASTLE (*aside*) Generous man! I now begin to
admire him. (*To him*) But I'm sure my family is as good as Miss
Hardcastle's, and though I'm poor, that's no great misfortune to
a contented mind, and until this moment I never thought that it
was bad to want fortune.

MARLOW. And why now, my pretty simplicity?

MISS HARDCASTLE. Because it puts me at a distance from one,
that if I had a thousand pounds I would give it all to.

MARLOW (*aside*) This simplicity bewitches me, so that if I
stay I'm undone. I must make one bold effort and leave her. (*To
her*) Your partiality in my favour, my dear, touches me most
sensibly and were I to live for myself alone, I could easily fix my
choice. But I owe too much to the opinion of the world, too much
to the authority of a father, so that—I can scarcely speak it—it
affects me. Farewell.

(MARLOW *exits*)

MISS HARDCASTLE. I never knew half his merit till now. He
shall not go, if I have power or art to detain him. I'll still preserve
the character in which I stooped to conquer, but will undeceive
my papa, who, perhaps, may laugh him out of his resolution.

(MISS HARDCASTLE *exits* L.
TONY *and* MISS NEVILLE *enter* R)

TONY. Ay, you may steal for yourselves the next time; I have
done my duty. She has got the jewels again, that's a sure thing;
but she believes it was all a mistake of the servants.

MISS NEVILLE. But, my dear cousin, sure you won't forsake us
in this distress. If she in the least suspects that I am going off, I
shall certainly be locked up, or sent to my Aunt Pedigree's, which
is ten times worse.

TONY. To be sure, aunts of all kinds are damned bad things.

But what can I do? I have got you a pair of horses that will fly like Whistlejacket, and I'm sure you can't say but I have courted you nicely before her face. Here she comes; we must court a bit or two more, for fear she should suspect us.

(*They move up stage and seem to fondle.*
MRS HARDCASTLE *enters* R)

MRS HARDCASTLE. Well, I was greatly fluttered, to be sure. But my son tells me it was all a mistake of the servants. I shan't be easy, however, till they are fairly married, and then let her keep her own fortune. But what do I see? Fondling together, as I'm alive. I never saw Tony so sprightly before. Ah, have I caught you, my pretty doves? What, billing, exchanging stolen glances, and broken murmurs! Ah!

TONY. As for murmurs, mother, we grumble a little now and then, to be sure. But there's no love lost between us.

MRS HARDCASTLE. A mere sprinkling, Tony, upon the flame, only to make it burn brighter.

MISS NEVILLE. Cousin Tony promises to give us more of his company at home. Indeed, he shan't leave us any more. It won't leave us, cousin Tony, will it?

TONY. Oh, it's a pretty creature! No, I'd sooner leave my horse in a pound than leave you when you smile upon one so. Your laugh makes you so becoming.

MISS NEVILLE. Agreeable cousin! Who can help admiring that natural humour, that pleasant, broad, red, thoughtless—(*patting his cheek*) ah, it's a bold face!

MRS HARDCASTLE. Pretty innocence!

TONY. I'm sure I always loved Cousin Con's hazel eyes, and her pretty long fingers, that she twists this way and that over the *haspicholls, like a parcel of bobbins.

MRS HARDCASTLE. Ah, he would charm the bird from the tree. I was never so happy before. My boy takes after his father, poor Mr Lumpkin, exactly. The jewels, my dear Con, shall be yours incontinently—you shall have them. Isn't he a sweet boy, my dear? You shall be married tomorrow, and we'll put off the rest of his education, like Dr Drowsy's sermons, to a fitter opportunity.

(DIGGORY *enters* L)

DIGGORY. Where's the 'squire? I have got a letter for your worship.

TONY. Give it to my mamma; she reads all my letters first.

DIGGORY. I had orders to deliver it into your own hands.

TONY. Who does it come from?

DIGGORY. Your worship mun ask that o' the letter itself.

(DIGGORY *exits* L)

* Haspicholls, *i.e. harpsichord.*

Tony. I could wish, to know, though. (*He turns the letter and gazes on it*)

Miss Neville (*aside*) Undone, undone! A letter to him from Hastings—I know the hand. If my aunt sees it, we are ruined for ever. I'll keep her employed a little if I can. (*To Mrs Hardcastle*) But I have not told you, madam, of my cousin's smart answer just now to Mr Marlow. We so laughed. You must know, madam —this way a little, for he must not hear us.

(*They go up stage and talk*)

Tony (*still gazing*) A damned cramp piece of penmanship as ever I saw in my life. I can read your print-hand very well, but here there are such handles, and shanks and dashes that one can scarce tell the head from the tail. "To Anthony Lumpkin, Esq." It's very odd, I can read the outside of my letters, where my own name is, well enough, but when I come to open it, it is all—buzz. That's hard, very hard; for the inside of the letter is always the cream of the correspondence.

Mrs Hardcastle (*aside to Miss Neville*) Ha, ha, ha!—very well, very well. And so my son was too hard for the philosopher.

Miss Neville (*aside to Mrs Hardcastle*) Yes, madam; but you must hear the rest, madam. A little more this way, or he may hear us. You'll hear how he puzzled him again.

Mrs Hardcastle (*aside to Miss Neville*) He seems strangely puzzled now himself, methinks.

Tony (*still gazing*) A confounded up and down hand, as if it was disguised in liquor. (*Reading*) "Dear Sir"—ay, that's that. Then there's an M, and a T, and a S; but whether the next be an izzard or a R, confound me, I cannot tell.

Mrs Hardcastle (*moving down*) What's that, my dear? Can I give you any assistance? (*She takes the letter*)

Miss Neville (*moving down*) Pray, aunt, let me read it. Nobody reads a cramp hand better than I. (*She twitches the letter from her*) Do you know who it is from?

Tony. Can't tell, except from Dick Ginger the *feeder.

Miss Neville. Ay, so it is. (*She pretends to read*) "Dear 'squire, —Hoping that you're in health, as I am at this present. The gentlemen of the Shakebag Club has cut the gentlemen of Goose-green quite out of feather. The odds—um—odd battle—um— long fighting—um . . ." here, here, it's all about cocks and fighting; it's of no consequence—here, put it up, put it up. (*She thrusts the crumpled letter upon him*)

Tony. But I tell you, miss, it's of all the consequence in the world. I would not lose the rest of it for a guinea. Here, Mother, do you make it out. Of no consequence! (*He gives Mrs Hardcastle the letter*)

Mrs Hardcastle. How's this. (*She reads*) "Dear 'squire,—I'm

* feeder, *i.e. cock-feeder and trainer.*

now waiting for Miss Neville, with a post-chaise and pair, at the bottom of the garden, but I find my horses yet unable to perform the journey. I expect you'll assist us with a pair of fresh horses, as you promised. Despatch is necessary, as the hag"—ay, the hag —"your mother, will otherwise suspect us. Yours, Hastings." Grant me patience! I shall run distracted! My rage chokes me!

MISS NEVILLE. I hope, madam, you'll suspend your resentment for a few moments, and not impute to me any impertinence or sinister design that belongs to another.

MRS HARDCASTLE (*curtsying very low*) Fine-spoken, madam; you are most miraculously polite and engaging, and quite the very pink of courtesy and circumspection, madam. (*Changing her tone*) And you, you great ill-fashioned oaf, with scarce sense enough to keep your mouth shut, were you, too, joined against me? But I'll defeat all your plots in a moment. As for you, madam, since you have got a pair of fresh horses ready, it would be cruel to disappoint them; so, if you please, instead of running away with your spark, prepare, this very moment, to run off with *me*. Your old Aunt Pedigree will keep you secure, I'll warrant me. You too, sir, may mount your horse, and guard us upon the way. Here, Thomas, Roger, Diggory. I'll show you that I wish you better than you do yourselves.

(MRS HARDCASTLE *exits* R)

MISS NEVILLE. So, now I'm completely ruined.

TONY. Ay, that's a sure thing.

MISS NEVILLE. What better could be expected from being connected with such a stupid fool—and after all the nods and signs I made him.

TONY. By the laws, miss, it was your own cleverness, and not my stupidity, that did your business. You were so nice and so busy with your Shakebags and Goose-greens, that I thought you could never be making believe.

(HASTINGS *enters* L)

HASTINGS. So, sir, I find by my servant that you have shown my letter and betrayed us. Was this well done, young gentleman?

TONY. Here's another. Ask miss there who betrayed you. Ecod, it was her doing, not mine. (*He seats himself on the table*)

(MARLOW *enters* R)

MARLOW. So I have been finely used here among you. Rendered contemptible, driven into ill-manners, despised, insulted, laughed at.

TONY. Here's another. We shall have old Bedlam broke loose presently.

MISS NEVILLE. And there, sir, is the gentleman to whom we all owe every obligation.

MARLOW. What can I say to him, a mere boy, an idiot, whose ignorance and age are a protection.

HASTINGS. A poor contemptible booby that would but disgrace correction.

MISS NEVILLE. Yet with cunning and malice enough to make himself merry with all our embarrassments.

HASTINGS. An insensible cub.

MARLOW. Replete with tricks and mischief.

TONY. Bah! (*He starts up*) Damme, but I'll fight you both, one after the other—with *baskets.

MARLOW. As for him, he's below resentment; but your conduct, Mr Hastings, requires an explanation. You knew of my mistakes, yet would not undeceive me.

HASTINGS. Tortured as I am with my own disappointments, is this a time for explanations? It is not friendly, Mr Marlow.

MARLOW. But sir . . .

MISS NEVILLE. Mr Marlow, we never kept on your mistake, till it was too late to undeceive you. Be pacified.

(*A* SERVANT *enters* R)

SERVANT. My mistress desires you'll get ready immediately, madam. The horses are putting to. Your hat and things are in the next room. We are to go thirty miles before morning.

(*The* SERVANT *exits* R)

MISS NEVILLE. Well, well; I'll come presently.

MARLOW. Was it well done, sir, to assist in rendering me ridiculous? To hang me out for the scorn of all my acquaintance? Depend upon it, sir, I shall expect an explanation.

HASTINGS. Was it well done, sir, if you're upon that subject, to deliver what I entrusted to yourself to the care of another, sir?

MISS NEVILLE. Mr Hastings. Mr Marlow. Why will you increase my distress by this groundless dispute? I implore, I entreat you . . .

(*The* SERVANT *enters* R *with a cloak*)

SERVANT. Your cloak, madam. My mistress is impatient.

MISS NEVILLE. I come.

(*The* SERVANT *exits* R)

Pray be pacified. If I leave you thus, I shall die with apprehension!

(*The* SERVANT *enters* R *with fan, muff and gloves*)

SERVANT. Your fan, muff and gloves, madam. The horses are waiting.

(*The* SERVANT *exits* R)

* Baskets, *i.e. single-sticks.*

MISS NEVILLE. Oh, Mr Marlow, if you knew what a scene of constraint and ill-nature lies before me, I'm sure it would convert your resentment into pity.

MARLOW. I'm so distracted with a variety of passions that I don't know what to do. Forgive me, madam. George, forgive me. You know my hasty temper, and should not exasperate it.

HASTINGS. The torture of my situation is my only excuse.

MISS NEVILLE. Well, my dear Hastings, if you have that esteem for me that I think, that I am sure you have, your constancy for three years will but increase the happiness of our future connexion. If . . .

MRS HARDCASTLE (*off* R)   Miss Neville! Constance! Why, Constance, I say.

MISS NEVILLE. I'm coming. Well, constancy. Remember, constancy is the word.

(MISS NEVILLE *exits* R)

HASTINGS. My heart, how can I support this! To be so near happiness, and such happiness.

MARLOW (*to Tony*)   You see now, young gentleman, the effects of your folly. What might be amusement to you is here disappointment, and even distress.

TONY (*from a reverie*)   Ecod, I have hit it!—it's here. Your hands: yours, and yours, my poor Sulky. (*He calls off*) My boots there, ho. Meet me two hours hence at the bottom of the garden; and if you don't find Tony Lumpkin a more good-natured fellow than you thought for, I'll give you leave to take my best horse and Bet Bouncer into the bargain. Come along. My boots, ho!

TONY *exits* R.

MARLOW *and* HARDCASTLE *exit* L *as—*

the CURTAIN *falls*

ACT V

Scene 1

SCENE—*The same.*

When the CURTAIN *rises,* HASTINGS *and a* SERVANT *enter* L.

HASTINGS. You saw the old lady and Miss Neville drive off, you say.

SERVANT. Yes, your honour. They went off in a post-coach, and the young 'squire went on horseback. They're thirty miles off by this time.

HASTINGS. Then all my hopes are over.

SERVANT. Yes, sir. Old Sir Charles has arrived. He and the old gentleman of the house have been laughing at Mr Marlow's mistake this half-hour. They are coming this way.

HASTINGS. Then I must not be seen. So now to my fruitless appointment at the bottom of the garden. This is about the time.

(HASTINGS *and the* SERVANT *exit* L.
HARDCASTLE *and* SIR CHARLES MARLOW *enter* R)

HARDCASTLE. Ha, ha, ha! The peremptory tone in which he sent forth his sublime commands.

SIR CHARLES. And the reserve with which, I suppose, he treated all your advances.

HARDCASTLE. And yet he might have seen something in me above a common innkeeper, too.

SIR CHARLES. Yes, Dick, but he mistook you for an *uncommon* innkeeper—ha, ha, ha!

HARDCASTLE. Well, I'm in too good spirits to think of anything but joy. Yes, my dear friend, this union of our families will make our personal friendships hereditary: and though my daughter's fortune is but small . . .

SIR CHARLES. Why, Dick, will you talk of fortune to *me?* My son is possessed of more than a competence already, and can want nothing but a good and virtuous girl to share his happiness and increase it. If they like each other, as you say they do . . .

HARDCASTLE. *If*, man! I tell you they *do* like each other—my daughter as good as told me so.

SIR CHARLES. But girls are apt to flatter themselves, you know.

HARDCASTLE. I saw him grasp her hand in the warmest manner myself; and here he comes to put you out of your ifs, I warrant him.

(MARLOW *enters* L)

MARLOW. I come, sir, once more, to ask pardon for my strange conduct. I can scarce reflect on my insolence without confusion.

HARDCASTLE. Tut, boy, a trifle. (*He shakes hands with him*) You take it too gravely. An hour or two's laughing with my daughter will set all to rights again; she'll never like you the worse for it.

MARLOW. Sir, I shall be always proud of her approbation.

HARDCASTLE. Approbation is but a cold word, Mr Marlow; if I am not deceived, you have something more than approbation thereabouts. You take me.

MARLOW. Really, sir, I have not that happiness.

HARDCASTLE. Come, boy, I'm an old fellow, and know what's what, as well as you that are younger. I know what has passed between you; but mum.

MARLOW. Sure, sir, nothing has passed between us but the most profound respect on my side and the most distant reserve on hers. You don't think, sir, that my impudence has been passed upon all the rest of the family?

HARDCASTLE. Impudence? No, I don't say that—not quite impudence—though girls like to be played with, and rumpled a little too, sometimes. But she has told no tales I assure you.

MARLOW. I never gave her the slightest cause.

HARDCASTLE. Well, well, I like modesty in its place well enough. But this is over-acting, young gentleman. You *may* be open. Your father and I will like you the better for it.

MARLOW. May I die, sir, if I ever . . .

HARDCASTLE. I tell you she don't dislike you; and as I'm sure you like her——

MARLOW. Dear sir, I protest, sir . . .

HARDCASTLE. I see no reason why you should not be joined as fast as the parson can tie you.

MARLOW. But hear me, sir . . .

HARDCASTLE. Your father approves the match, I admire it, every moment's delay will be doing mischief, so . . .

MARLOW. But why won't you hear me? By all that's just and true, I never gave Miss Hardcastle the slightest mark of my attachment, or even the most distant hint to suspect me of affection. We had but one interview, and that was formal, modest, and uninteresting.

HARDCASTLE (*aside*) This fellow's formal, modest impudence is beyond bearing.

SIR CHARLES. And you never grasped her hand, or made any protestations.

MARLOW. As heaven is my witness, I came down in obedience to your commands. I saw the lady without emotion and parted without reluctance. I hope you'll exact no further proofs of my duty, nor prevent me from leaving a house in which I suffer so many mortifications.

(MARLOW *exits* L)

SIR CHARLES. I'm astonished at the air of sincerity with which he parted.

HARDCASTLE. And I'm astonished at the deliberate intrepidity of his assurance.

SIR CHARLES. I dare pledge my life and honour upon his truth.

HARDCASTLE. Here comes my daughter, and I would stake my happiness upon her veracity.

(MISS HARDCASTLE *enters* R)

Kate, come hither, child.

(MISS HARDCASTLE *crosses to* C)

Answer us sincerely, and without reserve; has Mr Marlow made you any professions of love and affection?

MISS HARDCASTLE. The question is very abrupt, sir, but since you require unreserved sincerity, I think he has.

HARDCASTLE (*to Sir Charles*) You see.

SIR CHARLES. And pray, madam, have you and my son had more than one interview?

MISS HARDCASTLE. Yes, sir, several.

HARDCASTLE (*to Sir Charles*) You see.

SIR CHARLES. But did he profess any attachment?

MISS HARDCASTLE. A lasting one.

SIR CHARLES. Did he talk of love?

MISS HARDCASTLE. Much, sir.

SIR CHARLES. Amazing! And all this formally?

MISS HARDCASTLE. Formally.

HARDCASTLE. Now, my friend, I hope you are satisfied.

SIR CHARLES. And how did he behave, madam?

MISS HARDCASTLE. As most professed admirers do. Said some civil things of my face, talked much of *his* want of merit, and the greatness of *mine*; mentioned his heart, gave a short tragedy speech, and ended with pretended rapture.

SIR CHARLES. Now I'm perfectly convinced indeed. I know his conversation among women to be modest and submissive. This forward, canting, ranting manner by no means describes him, and I'm confident he never sat for the picture.

MISS HARDCASTLE. Then what, sir, if I should convince you to your face of my sincerity? If you and my papa, in about half an hour, will place yourselves behind that screen, you shall hear him declare his passion to me in person.

SIR CHARLES. Agreed. And if I find him what you describe, all my happiness in him must have an end.

(HARDCASTLE *and* SIR CHARLES *exit* R)

Miss Hardcastle. And if you *don't* find him what I describe, I fear my happiness must never have a beginning.

Miss Hardcastle *exits* l *as—*

the Curtain *falls*

Scene 2

Scene—*The garden of the house.*

When the Curtain *rises,* Hastings *enters* l.

Hastings. What an idiot am I, to wait here for a fellow who probably takes a delight in mortifying me. He never intended to be punctual, and I'll wait no longer. What do I see? It is he, and perhaps with news of Constance.

(Tony *enters up* l, *booted and spattered*)

My honest 'squire! I now find you a man of your word. This looks like friendship.

Tony. Ay, I'm your friend, and the best friend you have in the world, if you knew but all. This riding by night, by the bye, is cursedly tiresome. It has shook me worse than the basket of a stage-coach.

Hastings. But how—where did you leave your fellow travellers? Are they in safety? Are they housed?

Tony. Five-and-twenty miles in two hours and a half is no such bad driving. The poor beasts have smoked for it. Rabbet me, but I'd rather ride forty miles after a fox than ten with such varmint.

Hastings. Well, but where have you left the ladies? I die with impatience.

Tony. Left them? Why, where should I leave them, but where I found them?

Hastings. This is a riddle.

Tony. Riddle me this, then. What's that goes round the house and round the house, and never touches the house?

Hastings. I'm still astray.

Tony. Why, that's it, mun. I have led them astray. By Jingo! There's not a pond or slough within five miles of the place but they can tell the taste of.

Hastings. Ha, ha, ha! I understand: you took them in a round while they supposed themselves going forward. And so you have at last brought them home again.

Tony. You shall hear. I first took them down Featherbed Lane, where we stuck fast in the mud. I then rattled them crack over the stones of Up-and-down Hill. I then introduced them to the gibbet on Heavy-Tree Heath, and from that. with a *circum-bendibus*, I fairly lodged them in the horse-pond at the bottom of the garden.

HASTINGS. But no accident, I hope?

TONY. No, no; only Mother is confoundedly frightened. She thinks herself forty miles off. She's sick of the journey, and the cattle can scarce crawl. So if your own horses be ready, you may whip off with cousin, and I'll be bound that no soul here can budge a foot to follow you.

HASTINGS. My dear friend, how can I be grateful?

TONY. Ay, now it's dear friend, noble 'squire. Just now it was all idiot, cub, and run me through the body. Damn your way of fighting, I say. After we take a knock in this part of the country we shake hands and be friends; but if you had run me through the guts then I should be dead, and you might go kiss the hangman.

HASTINGS. The rebuke is just. But I must hasten to relieve Miss Neville; if you keep the old lady employed, I promise to take care of the young one.

TONY. Never fear me. Here she comes. Vanish.

(HASTINGS *exits* L)

She's got from the pond, and draggled up to the waist like a mermaid.

(MRS HARDCASTLE *enters up* L)

MRS HARDCASTLE. Oh, Tony, I'm killed—shook—battered to death! I shall never survive it. That last jolt that laid us against the quick-set hedge has done my business.

TONY. Alack, mamma, it was all your fault. You would be for running away by night, without knowing one inch of the way.

MRS HARDCASTLE. I wish we were at home again. I never met so many accidents in so short a journey. Drenched in the mud, overturned in a ditch, stuck fast in a slough, jolted to a jelly, and at last to lose our way. Whereabouts do you think we are, Tony?

TONY. By my guess we should be upon Crackskull Common about forty miles from home.

MRS HARDCASTLE. O lud! O lud! The most notorious spot in all the country. We only want a robbery to make a complete night on't.

TONY. Don't be afraid, mamma, don't be afraid. Two of the five that kept here are hanged, and the other three may not find us. Don't be afraid. Is that a man that's galloping behind us? No; it's only a tree. Don't be afraid.

MRS HARDCASTLE. The fright will certainly kill me.

TONY. Do you see anything like a black hat moving behind the thicket?

MRS HARDCASTLE. Oh, death!

TONY. No, it's only a cow. Don't be afraid, Mamma—don't be afraid.

MRS HARDCASTLE. As I'm alive, Tony, I see a man coming towards us—ah, I'm sure on't! If he perceives us we are undone.

TONY (*aside*) Father-in-law, by all that's unlucky, come to take one of his night walks. (*To her*) Ah, it's a highwayman with pistols as long as my arm. A damned ill-looking fellow.

MRS HARDCASTLE. Good heaven defend us! He approaches.

TONY. Do you hide yourself in that thicket, and leave me to manage him. If there be any danger, I'll cough and cry hem. When I cough, be sure to keep close.

(MRS HARDCASTLE *hides behind a tree up stage.*
     HARDCASTLE *enters down* R)

HARDCASTLE. I'm mistaken, or I heard voices of people in want of help. Oh, Tony, is that you? I did not expect you so soon back. Are your mother and her charge in safety?

TONY. Very safe, sir, at my Aunt Pedigree's. Hem! (*He coughs*)

MRS HARDCASTLE (*from behind*) Ah, death! I find there's danger.

HARDCASTLE. Forty miles in three hours; sure that's too much, my youngster.

TONY. Stout horses and willing minds make short journeys, as they say. Hem! (*He coughs*)

MRS HARDCASTLE (*from behind*) Sure he'll do the dear boy no harm.

HARDCASTLE. But I heard a voice here; I should be glad to know from whence it came.

TONY. It was I, sir, talking to myself, sir. I was saying that forty miles in three hours was very good going. Hem! As to be sure it was. Hem! I have got a sort of cold by being out in the air. We'll go in, if you please. Hem!

HARDCASTLE. But if you talked to yourself, you did not answer yourself. I am certain I heard two voices, and am resolved (*raising his voice*) to find the other out.

MRS HARDCASTLE (*from behind*) Oh, he's coming to find me out. Oh!

TONY. What need you go, sir, if I tell you? Hem! I'll lay down my life for the truth. Hem! I'll tell you all, sir. (*He detains him*)

HARDCASTLE. I tell you I will not be detained. I insist on seeing. It's in vain to expect I'll believe you.

MRS HARDCASTLE (*rushing forward*, C) O lud, he'll murder my poor boy, my darling! Here, good gentleman, whet your rage upon me. Take my money, my life, but spare that young gentleman, spare my child, if you have any mercy.

HARDCASTLE. My wife, as I'm a Christian! From whence can she come, or what does she mean!

MRS HARDCASTLE (*kneeling*) Take compassion on us, good Mr Highwayman; take our money, our watches, all we have, but spare our lives. We will never bring you to justice, indeed we won't, good Mr Highwayman.

HARDCASTLE. I believe the woman's out of her senses. What, Dorothy, don't you know *me*?

MRS HARDCASTLE. Mr Hardcastle, as I'm alive! My fears blinded me. But who, my dear, could have expected to meet you here, in this frightful place, so far from home? What has brought you to follow us?

HARDCASTLE. Sure, Dorothy, you have not lost your wits. "So far from home", when you are within forty yards of your own door. (*To Tony*) This is one of your old tricks, you graceless rogue you. (*To Mrs Hardcastle*) Don't you know the gate and the mulberry tree; and don't you remember the horse-pond, my dear?

MRS HARDCASTLE. Yes, I shall remember the horse-pond as long as I live; I have caught my death in't. (*To Tony*) And is it to you, you graceless varlet, I owe all this? I'll teach you to abuse your Mother, I will.

TONY. Ecod, mother, all the parish say you have spoiled me, and so you may take the fruits on't.

MRS HARDCASTLE. I'll spoil you, I will.

(MRS HARDCASTLE *chases* TONY *off* R)

HARDCASTLE. There's morality, however, in his reply.

(*He exits* R.
HASTINGS *and* MISS NEVILLE *enter* L)

HASTINGS. My dear Constance, why will you deliberate thus? If we delay a moment, all is lost for ever. Pluck up a little resolution, and we shall soon be out of the reach of her malignity.

MISS NEVILLE. I find it impossible. My spirits are so sunk with the agitations I have suffered that I am unable to face any new danger. Two or three years' patience will at last crown us with happiness.

HASTINGS. Such a tedious delay is worse than inconstancy. Let us fly, my charmer. Let us date our happiness from this very moment. Perish fortune; love and content will increase what we possess beyond a monarch's revenue. Let me prevail.

MISS NEVILLE. No, Mr Hastings, no. Prudence once more comes to my relief, and I will obey its dictates. In the moment of passion, fortune may be despised, but it ever produces a lasting repentance. I'm resolved to apply to Mr Hardcastle's compassion and justice for redress.

HASTINGS. But though he had the will, he has not the power to relieve you.

MISS NEVILLE. But he has influence, and upon that I am resolved to rely.

Hastings. I have no hopes. But since you persist I must reluctantly obey you.

Hastings *and* Miss Neville *exit* L *as—*

the Curtain *falls*

Scene 3

Scene—*Inside the house.*

When the Curtain *rises,* Sir Charles, Marlow *and* Miss Hardcastle *enter* L.

Sir Charles. What a situation am I in! If what you say appears, I shall then find a guilty son. If what he says be true, I shall then lose one that, of all others, I most wished for, a daughter.

Miss Hardcastle. I am proud of your approbation, and to show I merit it, if you place yourselves as I directed, you shall hear his explicit declaration. But he comes.

Sir Charles. I'll to your father, and keep him to the appointment.

(Sir Charles *exits* R.
    Marlow *enters* L)

Marlow. Though prepared for setting out, I come once more to take leave; nor did I, till this moment know the pain I feel in the separation.

Miss Hardcastle (*in her own natural manner*) I believe these sufferings cannot be very great, sir, which you can so easily remove. A day or two longer, perhaps, might lessen your uneasiness, by showing the little value of what you now think proper to regret.

Marlow (*aside*) This girl every moment improves upon me. (*To her*) It must not be, madam. I have already trifled too long with my heart; my very pride begins to submit to my passion. The disparity of education and fortune, the anger of a parent, and the contempt of my equals begin to lose their weight, and nothing can restore me to myself but this painful effort of resolution.

Miss Hardcastle. Then go, sir. I'll urge nothing more to detain you. Though my family be as good as hers you came down to visit, and my education I hope not inferior, what are these advantages without equal affluence? I must remain contented with the slight approbation of imputed merit; I must have only the mockery of your addresses, while all your serious aims are fixed on fortune.

(Sir Charles *and* Hardcastle *enter unseen up* R)

SIR CHARLES. Here, behind this screen.

HARDCASTLE. Ay, ay, make no noise. I'll engage my Kate covers him with confusion at last.

MARLOW. By heaven, madam, fortune was ever my smallest consideration. Your beauty at first caught my eye, for who could see that without emotion? But every moment that I converse with you steals in some new grace, heightens the picture, and gives it stronger expression. What at first seemed rustic plainness now appears refined simplicity. What seemed forward assurance now strikes me as the result of courageous innocence and conscious virtue.

SIR CHARLES. What can it mean? He amazes me!

HARDCASTLE. I told you how it would be. Hush!

MARLOW. I am now determined to stay, madam, and I have too good an opinion of my father's discernment when he sees you, to doubt his approbation.

MISS HARDCASTLE. No, Mr Marlow, I will not, cannot detain you. Do you think I could suffer a connexion in which there is the smallest room for repentance? Do you think I would take the mean advantage of a transient passion to load you with confusion? Do you think I could ever relish that happiness which was acquired by lessening yours?

MARLOW. By all that's good, I can have no happiness but what's in your power to grant me. Nor shall I ever feel repentance but in not having seen your merits before. I will stay, even contrary to your wishes; and though you should persist to shun me, I will make my respectful assiduities atone for the levity of my past conduct.

MISS HARDCASTLE. Sir, I must entreat you'll desist. As our acquaintance began, so let it end, in indifference. I might have given an hour or two to levity, but seriously, Mr Marlow, do you think I could ever submit to a connexion where *I* must appear mercenary and *you* imprudent? Do you think I could ever catch at the confident address of a secure admirer?

MARLOW (*kneeling*) Does this look like security? Does this look like confidence? No, madam, every moment that shows me your merit only serves to increase my diffidence and confusion. Here let me continue . . .

SIR CHARLES. I can hold it no longer. (*He comes forward*, C) Charles, Charles, how have you deceived me! Is this your indifference, your uninteresting conversation?

HARDCASTLE (*moving* RC) Your cold contempt? Your formal interview? What have you to say now?

MARLOW. That I'm all amazement! What can it mean?

HARDCASTLE. It means that you can say and unsay things at pleasure. That you can address a lady in private and deny it in public; that you have one story for us and another for my daughter.

MARLOW. Daughter!—this lady your daughter!

HARDCASTLE. Yes, sir, my only daughter, my Kate. Whose else should she be?

MARLOW. Oh, the devil!

MISS HARDCASTLE. Yes, sir, that very identical tall, squinting lady you were pleased to take me for. (*She curtsies*) She that you addressed as the mild, modest, sentimental man of gravity, and the bold, forward, agreeable Rattle of the Ladies' Club—ha, ha, ha!

MARLOW. Zounds! there's no bearing this; it's worse than death.

MISS HARDCASTLE. In which of your characters, sir, will you give us leave to address you? (*She mimics him*) As the faltering gentleman, with looks on the ground, that speaks just to be heard, and hates hypocrisy; or the loud, confident creature, that keeps it up with Mrs Mantrap and old Miss Biddy Buckskin till three in the morning—ha, ha, ha!

MARLOW. Oh, curse on my noisy head! I never attempted to be impudent yet that I was not taken down. I must be gone.

HARDCASTLE. By the hand of my body, but you shall not. I see it was all a mistake, and I am rejoiced to find it. You shall not, sir, I tell you—I know she'll forgive you. Won't you forgive him, Kate? We'll all forgive you. Take courage, man.

(MARLOW *and* MISS HARDCASTLE *move up stage, she tormenting him.*
        MRS HARDCASTLE *and* TONY *enter* L)

MRS HARDCASTLE. So, so they're gone off. Let them go—I care not. (*She crosses to* R)

HARDCASTLE. Who's gone?

MRS HARDCASTLE. My dutiful niece and her gentleman, Mr Hastings, from town. He who came down with our modest visitor here.

SIR CHARLES. Who! my honest George Hastings? As worthy a fellow as lives, and the girl could not have made a more prudent choice.

HARDCASTLE. Then by the hand of my body, I'm proud of the connexion.

MRS HARDCASTLE. Well, if he has taken away the lady, he has not taken her fortune; that remains in this family to console us for her loss.

HARDCASTLE. Sure, Dorothy, you would not be so mercenary?

MRS HARDCASTLE. Ay, that's my affair, not yours.

HARDCASTLE. But you know, if your son, when of age, refuses to marry his cousin, her whole fortune is then at her own disposal.

MRS HARDCASTLE. Ay, but he's not of age, and she has not thought proper to wait for his refusal.

(HASTINGS *and* MISS NEVILLE *enter* L)

Mrs Hardcastle (aside) What, returned so soon? I begin not to like it.

Hastings (to Hardcastle) For my late attempt to fly off with your niece, let my present confusion be my punishment. We are now come back to appeal from your justice to your humanity. By her father's consent, I first paid her my addresses, and our passions were first founded in duty.

Miss Neville. Since his death I have been obliged to stoop to dissimulation to avoid oppression. In an hour of levity I was ready even to give up my fortune to secure my choice. But I'm now recovered from the delusion, and hope from your tenderness what is denied me from a nearer connexion.

Mrs Hardcastle. Pshaw, pshaw, this is all but the whining end of a modern novel.

Hardcastle. Be it what it will, I'm glad they're come back to reclaim their due. Come hither, Tony, boy. Do you refuse this lady's hand whom I now offer you?

Tony. What signifies my refusing. You know I can't refuse her till I'm of age, father.

Hardcastle. While I thought concealing your age, boy, was likely to conduce to your improvement, I concurred with your mother's desire to keep it secret; but since I find she turns it to a wrong use, I must now declare you have been of age these three months.

Tony. Of age! Am I of age, father?

Hardcastle. Above three months.

Tony. Then you'll see the first use I'll make of my liberty. (He takes Miss Neville's hand) Witness all men, by these presents, that I, Anthony Lumpkin, Esquire, of blank place, refuse you, Constantia Neville, spinster of no place at all, for my true and lawful wife. So Constance Neville may marry whom she pleases, and Tony Lumpkin is his own man again.

Sir Charles. O brave 'squire!

Hastings. My worthy friend!

Mrs Hardcastle. My undutiful offspring!

(Mrs Hardcastle beats Tony off L)

Marlow. Joy, my dear George, I give you joy sincerely. And could I prevail upon my little tyrant here to be less arbitrary, I should be the happiest man alive, if you would return me the favour.

Hastings (to Miss Hardcastle) Come, madam, you are now driven to the very last scene of all your contrivances. I know you like him, I'm sure he loves you, and you must and shall have him.

Hardcastle (joining their hands) And I say so too. And, Mr Marlow, if she makes as good a wife as she has a daughter, I don't believe you'll ever repent your bargain. So now to supper. To-

morrow we shall gather all the poor of the parish about us, and
the mistakes of the night shall be crowned with a merry morning.
So, boy, take her; and as you have been mistaken in the mistress,
my wish is, that you may never be mistaken in the wife.

CURTAIN

EPILOGUE

BY DR GOLDSMITH

Well, having stooped to conquer with success,
And gained a husband without aid from dress,
Still, as a Barmaid, I could wish it too,
As I have conquered him to conquer you;
And let me say, for all your resolution,
That pretty Barmaids have done execution.
Our life is all a play, composed to please,
"We have our exits and our entrances."
The first act shows the simple country maid,
Harmless and young, of everything afraid;
Blushes when hired, and with unmeaning action,
I hopes as how to give you satisfaction.
Her second act displays a livelier scene,——
Th' unblushing Barmaid of a country inn:
Who whisks about the house, at market caters,
Talks loud, coquets the guests, and scolds the waiters.
Next the scene shifts to town, and there she soars,
The chop-house toast of ogling connoisseurs;
On 'Squires and Cits she there displays her arts,
And on the gridiron broils her lovers' hearts;
And as she smiles, her triumphs to complete,
Even Common Councilmen forget to eat.
The fourth act shows her wedded to the 'Squire,
And Madam now begins to hold it higher;
Pretends to taste, at Operas cries caro,
And quits her Nancy Dawson *for* Che Faro;
Dotes upon dancing, and in all her pride
Swims round the room, the *Heinel *of Cheapside;*
Ogles and leers with artificial skill,
Till, having lost in age the power to kill,
She sits all night at cards, and ogles at spadille.
Such, through our lives the eventful history
The fifth and last act still remains for me.
The Barmaid now for your protection prays,
Turns Female Barrister, and pleads for Bayes.

* Heinel, a French dancer.

EPILOGUE

To be spoken in the character of Tony Lumpkin

By J. Craddock Esq.

Well—now all's ended—and my comrades gone,
Pray what becomes of *mother's nonly son?*
A hopeful blade!—in town I'll fix my station,
And try to make a bluster in the nation.
As for my cousin Neville, I renounce her,
Off—in a crack—I'll carry big Bet Bouncer.
   Why should not I in the great world appear?
I soon shall have a thousand pounds a year;
No matter what a man may here inherit,
In London—'gad, they've some regard to spirit.
I see the horses prancing up the streets,
And big Bet Bouncer bobs to all she meets;
Then hoikes to jigs and pastimes ev'ry night—
Not to the plays—they say it a'n't polite;
To Sadler's Wells perhaps, or operas go,
And once, by chance, to the roratorio.
Thus here and there, for ever up and down,
We'll set the fashions, too, to half the town;
And then at auctions—money ne'er regard,
Buy pictures like the great, ten pounds a yard:
Zounds, we shall make these London gentry say,
We know what's damn'd genteel, as well as they.

This Epilogue was not spoken at the first production. For the history of the two Epilogues see page vi.